Advance Praise for
Circle of Impact

"This is a personal, generous, useful book, a chance to think deeply about the difference any of us can make. Right here and right now we can uplift those around us."

—SETH GODIN, author of *Linchpin*

CIRCLE OF
IMPACT

CIRCLE OF IMPACT

TAKING PERSONAL
INITIATIVE TO IGNITE CHANGE

DR. ED BRENEGAR

A SAVIO REPUBLIC BOOK
An Imprint of Post Hill Press

Circle of Impact:
Taking Personal Initiative to Ignite Change
© 2018 by Dr. Ed Brenegar
All Rights Reserved

ISBN: 978-1-68261-786-1
ISBN (eBook): 978-1-68261-787-8

Cover Design by The Keynote Group/Kim Hall
Interior Design and Composition by Greg Johnson, Textbook Perfect

posthillpress.com
New York • Nashville

Published in the United States of America

To my children who inspire me.
Troop and Jina,
Stewart,
and
Shelby.

With gratitude for your love and example.
Fran and Jane,
Frances and Ed,
and
Helen, Allen, and AHB, Sr.

TABLE OF CONTENTS

PREFACE

As the idea of this book was forming in my mind, I had a dream about being thrust into a situation of fear.

I'm in a cab. Not sure where I am going. The vehicle stops. I am greeted by a young woman who says, *"We've been waiting on you. You are up next."* She escorts me into a large auditorium.

I ask her, *"What am I doing here?"* She says, *"You are the next presenter."*

"What? I can't be. I'm not prepared. Who are these people? Why are they here? Why am I here? What am I supposed to say?"

"Just follow me to the stage." I walk up onto the platform. I turn and face the audience. I'm shaking. I stand there for what seems like an eternity. I'm looking out at several thousand people, and they at me. The auditorium is quiet. I look into their faces. Some are smiling. Some look worried. I begin to speak.

"Many of you sitting out there today wonder what it is like to stand here in front of all of you. It is frightening. Five minutes ago, I had no idea that I would be standing here in front of you.

"If you were in my shoes, what would you do? Run? For some reason, I don't feel I can run away from this.

"All I can tell you is that somewhere down deep inside of us is a story that has brought each of us to this stage of our lives. Our stories help us to see that there is some desire within us that defines our lives. It helps us to see that for our story to reach its completion that we must be willing to give ourselves to this story.

"All you have to do, as I am doing right now, is to tell that story as it lives in you. Let me tell you my story about what matters to me and is now the focus of my life and work."

I relax a moment, take a deep breath, and begin to tell them about who I am and what is important to me.

"I am a writer, a speaker, a coach, a father, a lover of art, books, music, film, and travel. I am a guy who is curious about everything. I want to make sense of a world that doesn't make much sense.

"I am a guy who believes in people so that they can believe in themselves.

"I believe in people because I see in them untapped, unrealized, undeveloped potential. Along with that, I see that much of the conflict, unhappiness, and pain that we experience is because we have never found that right path to fulfilling our potential.

"I believe that we have desires within us, where we long for meaning and purpose.

"If we were to practically connect with them, our lives and the lives of others would change for the better.

"I am not an idealist. I am a positive realist. I know that life can be hard, hurtful, and disappointing. If we don't manage our expectations, we can easily be beat down so that we never try to fulfill the desires that form the core of who we are.

Preface

"I am a leader for leaders. I care about and support people who lead from the roles that they have within their organizations and in society at large. For many of us, the choice of organizational leadership is a lonely journey. If this is your experience, I want to journey beside you in your desire to lead your people and organization.

"I see the world of leadership differently than most people. I don't see leadership as a title or a role in an organization. Instead, it is about how people function in their lives, about the difference they can make. I don't divide the world up into leaders and followers. We need to know how to be both. Leadership isn't a position of authority, but of personal responsibility. It is best practiced in a social setting where people share the responsibility for leadership. I believe we live in a leadership-starved world, and the future belongs to leader-rich organizations and societies.

"I believe the world of leadership is in crisis and conflict. The term 'leadership' has come to define a small, elite, entitled segment of the world's population. It has been institutionalized in organizations that make access to power and resources more difficult. People tell me that they don't want to be called a leader because of this institutional bias. This must change.

"I believe that anyone, regardless of who they are, where they come from, the pedigree of their education or total lack of it, can lead by taking initiative to create impact. A person isn't a leader because they take action. It is the character of their actions that defines them as a leader. Character is defined by why you lead and how you go about it. Leadership is defined by the difference you make that matters.

"Let me ask you a simple question.

"*Today, at this point in your life, what do you want to change? What is that one thing that has a hold on you, that won't let go because it's calling you to do something about it? What's stopping you from doing something about it today?*

"*The first great obstacle to overcome is in our self-perception of what is possible.*

"*I believe that there is only one measure for leadership. What changes because of you doing something? Without change, there is no impact, and impact is the core measure of leadership. Impact is change. Creating that impact is what leadership is all about.*

"*I believe that all leadership begins with personal initiative, a decision an individual makes to create impact.*

"*The practice of leadership is a relational one. We don't lead by ourselves, but with one another. It has always been this way.*

"*I believe that we are in a transition in human history that is unprecedented. The way societies and organizations have developed over the past two millennia has run its course. With the advent of the digital age, we now have the tools, knowledge, and resources to act upon our desires to create, innovate, and collaborate in ways not available to anyone before now.*

"*Part of this transition is a transformation of human purpose. Do we define ourselves by the roles that we serve in the institutions? Or, do we define ourselves by the impact that we seek to create through those roles?*

"*This transformation has everything to do with how we give ourselves to one another, and the difference that makes. It is about how we live together, work together, change together, and lead together. It is not about what I want to have, but rather what we can create together.*

Preface

"I believe all growth starts small. So, we start small. Small initiatives. Small changes. Small steps of building relationships of shared responsibility, beginning locally and extending globally. From those small steps, momentum grows, and the speed of change and the impact that follows accelerates."

Then I wake from my dream. I'm still standing on the stage. But now the audience of thousands is standing with me.

Are you of one of those who knows that there is something about you that has yet to be discovered, calling you out to change your life by changing other people's lives?

Join me on this journey, and may you wake from your own dream to discover that there is a life of impact waiting to be created.

INTRODUCTION

It may not surprise you, but we are living in a world in transition. We are saying,

> *We are all in transition,*
> *both personally and organizationally.*

This is not some random, disruptive, chaotic change we are experiencing. Instead, this is a long series of integrated changes that represent a dramatic transition in how we understand ourselves and the way the world functions.

I am not exactly saying it is futile to resist. However, I do think that it makes more sense to understand that the changes that are happening are for a reason. If we can understand this transition from that perspective, we can see an opportunity to be somebody, and do something through our organizations, which is historic.

I began to see this transition four decades ago. The Circle of Impact model of leadership is the outcome of my engagement in this transition over the years.

The Circle of Impact began as a simple idea about leadership. *All leadership begins with personal initiative.*

Anyone can take personal initiative. We all do it every day. We do things. We start things. We finish things. While we all take initiative, not all the actions we take are leadership ones.

If leadership begins with personal initiative, then we are saying something more significant. We are saying, *All leadership begins with personal initiative that makes a difference that matters.*

Now we are saying that leadership has an outcome that anyone can have.

What, then, does it mean to make a difference? It means that some change happens because of our personal initiative. An intentional act of change is an act for creating impact.

We are now saying, *All leadership begins with personal initiative that creates impact that makes a difference that matters.*

This is my point of departure from the traditional view of leadership. The conventional view, which has generally been accepted by everyone for decades, sees leadership as a rare, elite, even heroic function of a select group of people who tend to run organizations. I see something very different.

In the pages that follow, we'll look deeply into why and how this older perspective on leadership is in transition. Just as organizations and societies are changing, the leadership that is needed is changing. And we are changing along with it.

One of the reasons for this shift in perspective about leadership is that the conditions that supported the traditional way of leading have changed. It wasn't a kind of one-off change where things returned to the way they used to be. Instead, we are experiencing a series of changes in our world, which are taking us to a new place. This transition brings both anxiety and

hope. The greatest of these changes is in our own self-perception of what is possible for us to create and achieve personally
and together.

Just so you know, I didn't come at this idea of our being
in transition without some reluctance. The change that I see
happening in our lives, our local communities, and across the
world means that much of what we have found to be safe and
secure in the world is changing. Instead of jumping up and
down and celebrating this change in our world, I really want us
to approach this transition with seriousness and purposeful-
ness. While I do think the transition is going to be hard for a lot
of people and institutions, I also think that in the long run, it is
in everyone's best interest. It doesn't mean the future is rosy. I
see it filled with conflict and hard moral choices.

However, if we put into practice the perspective of the Circle
of Impact that you will find in this book, then our world won't
be starved for leaders, but instead will be a leader-rich one. The
best thing we can do is to learn to take personal responsibility for
what is within our control. I have designed the Circle of Impact
to help people live their lives, operate their organizations, and
care for their communities in simple, practical ways.

In the chapters that follow, we will explore what the Circle of
Impact is, and just what it means that we are in transition.

The Focus of the Book

Circle of Impact: Taking Personal Initiative To Ignite Change
is divided into four sections. Each section takes on a specific
theme related to what it means to be a leader of impact in a
world of change.

In *Part One: All Leadership Begins with Personal Initiative*, I describe the Circle of Impact model of leadership, as well as explore personal and organizational leadership.

In *Part Two: We Are All in Transition*, I provide a perspective on change that I hope brings insight into not only why things are as they are in the world, but also how we can deal with change both personally and organizationally.

In *Part Three: Inside the Circle of Impact*, I show how to take the three dimensions of leadership and the four connecting ideas of the Circle of Impact and use them to bring wholeness and order to organizations. These two frameworks help us align the whole of our organizations for impact.

In the last section, *Part Four: Leadership Impact for a World in Transition*, I look at how to apply the Circle of Impact in organizations amid a global transition. The book has been written to change our perception of leadership, doing so in a simple, practical way.

Throughout the book are stories. Almost all the stories are fictionalized accounts of situations that I've witnessed or been involved in. I do this to isolate a particular part of the situation for the lesson of the chapter.

Starting Over

In the months prior to making the decision to write this book, I was at a transition point in my life. I was asking questions that you may have asked yourself at some point in your life. My transition point had me looking at decisions about where I would live, how I would financially support myself, and what difference I would make with the rest of my life. These decisions followed

Introduction

a time of loss where my consulting practice slowly dried up, and then, after moving from being a board member into the executive director role, I was terminated from the nonprofit organization that I led. During this time, my marriage of thirty years ended.

Looking back, I had reasons to doubt myself, as well as reasons to take pride in the work that I had done. What was missing was a sense of completeness about my life and career, in particular wondering what my life's legacy would be. I could have easily accepted a small, unambitious life, leading to retirement. I had people in my life who cared about me, who believed in me, and stood with me as I went through my season of loss. I have not had a bad or failed life, nor one filled with regrets or a longing for some unattainable success. My life has been as normal as normal can be. I have no reason to feel sorry for myself or wallow in self-pity.

Sitting in my apartment one night, the question of what my life was to be in the future became crystal clear to me. I saw myself starting over. I realized that my life was not done, there was much to do, and that my best, most important work was yet to be. So that evening, I decided that for me to start my life over, I had to move. Over the next few months, I would leave my home in North Carolina, where I had been born and raised, and move to Jackson Hole, Wyoming, where I knew only two people, to begin a new phase of my life and work. From that moment to right now, my journey has been one of self-discovery and the receiving of the kind and wise impact of people that I've met around the world. I'm grateful to those people who have joined me in my journey to bring the Circle of Impact to you.

My Audacious Goal

As I started over in almost every aspect of my life, my Circle of Impact model of leadership grew in significance and practicality. For two decades my purpose was *"To inspire leadership initiative"* by living my life with integrity as one of my core values. It brought me to ask myself, *"What should be the measure of my impact?"* Is it selling a lot of books, becoming a professional speaker, or becoming a recognized expert on 21st-century leadership? Each of those measures would be personally gratifying. But, they are not the measure of my impact.

If impact is change, then, *"What is the level of impact that I want to create, that would make a difference that would matter long after I've passed from this earth?"*

One percent. One percent of what?

I'll know that I have achieved the impact that I seek when I see one percent of the world's population take personal initiative to create leadership impact. That is 3.5 million people in the United States and seventy-five million worldwide taking action to make a difference in their local communities. The ripple effect will be a collective wisdom of learning to solve problems, create new opportunities, and create a better world from the ground up. More important to me, it means that the most insignificant person in any place, organization, or social group can, by their own actions, change the world.

Think about the lowliest, most invisible person you know personally. Imagine them doing something that makes a difference to someone, just as small and insignificant in the world's eyes. What would it be like if one percent of all people worldwide found a person who believed that they could have a significant impact in their local community? The world would change for the better overnight. I've known people like this who have had an impact on a small segment of the world. Our world is far more resilient in the face of change because of them.

Ironically, I have had people suggest that my goal is too big. They tell me it is egotistical to think that I can move seventy-five million people to take action. The reality is that egotists don't have audacious goals. They set their goals low enough to satisfy their ego. Audacious goals require people to give up their ego to call other people to join them. I know that moving one percent of the world to action is a ridiculous idea. However, we only think this because we are afraid that if we try, we might not make it. We have to lay aside our egos and fears because it just may be that one percent is too *small* a goal for the Circle of Impact.

When I decided to scale my life's impact, I had to build a team of people to join me. I especially am grateful for Yolanda and her team at The Keynote Group; for Nena and Austin at Dupree Miller; for Bill and our group of the Lion's Pride; for David and Donna, Seth, Tanya, Kurt, Sandy, Liza, Natalie, and Jim. Each of you, in your genius, has freed me to seek the impossible dream.

Lastly, as you begin to read *Circle of Impact*, I don't want you to think of this as an intellectual exercise in learning some new concepts about leadership. It is that, but it's also much more. I want you to see that you are being invited into a journey of self-discovery and personal change. That has been my experience in writing it. This change takes place within each of us, but it is not about us. It is for all those people out there in the world who are looking for people like you and me to show up and create the impact that awaits our decision to take personal initiative. When we do, we can each stand and say, with humility, *"Impact Starts with Me."*

PART ONE

ALL LEADERSHIP BEGINS WITH PERSONAL INITIATIVE

(1)

THE CIRCLE OF IMPACT—
A MODEL FOR LEADERS

Why Some Problems Never Get Solved

In the mid-1990s, I started my consulting practice with the aim of helping leaders strengthen their organizations, with the larger goal of strengthening their local communities. As one project after another came, a pattern began to emerge. Problems presented to me often turned out to be symptoms of more complex problems. These were not isolated incidents. The situations and the types of organizations were not similar. Their problems were similar. But more importantly, they were not getting resolved by the way we have all learned to solve problems. For as long as I've been working in organizations, the belief has been that the solution is in the problem itself. This approach failed to consider that there is always more going on than the problem itself.

The more significant pattern that I saw was that leaders' perspectives were fragmented. They were not able to see their organizations as a whole. To put it differently, they were not able to see how the parts of their organizations fit together as an integrated whole. It wasn't that they couldn't see how one part influenced another. The problem was that there wasn't a simple perspective that could be practiced by everyone in the organization. Fragmented thinking produces more of the same. Here is an example of what I mean.

Communication is always an easily identified problem. It is often used as the reason why a client or a team member did not respond the way we expected them to respond. Too often it is how we understand the delivery of information to the public or what we mean when we send a survey to a group seeking their input. As one who has used surveys to gather perspective for clients, I always produced a report that could be distributed to the responders. It is an issue of respect and trust for me. It was a rare occasion when I'd receive one from a survey I'd completed. There is good reason why communication is the organizational problem at the top of my list.

If communication is a problem in your organization, what kind of problem is it? Is it poorly articulated information lacking a clear call to action? Is it a badly designed approach for getting information into the right hands so that they will pay attention to it? Is it a lack of understanding about the kind of information the recipient wants from you? Is it that the information sounds too generic, as if the leadership team is not in touch with the realities of the client? Or is the basic problem in our thinking that communication is simply the delivery of information to the marketplace?

While addressing this recurring problem with clients, the Circle of Impact developed. The issue of communication is a multidimensional one. The Circle of Impact came into existence

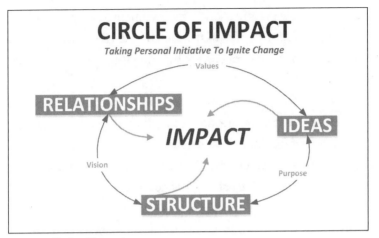

Figure 1. Circle of Impact

to help people, like you and me, find a simple, practical way to address the complex situations of human communication that we daily encounter in our personal and professional lives.

The Circle of Impact is a dynamic picture of the interaction among three aspects of an organization—ideas, relationships, and structure—called the three dimensions of leadership. Typically, these three areas are treated separately. We don't even see how they interact and influence one another. At best, we see how they get in the way of the real business of the organization.

In particular, this is true regarding how the operation of the organizational structure tends to diminish the importance of people in relationship with one another. In addition, ideas, like values, get marginalized as marketing words—*"Your trusted provider of..."*—instead of as strategic insights for developing the long-range strength and sustainability of the company. In a structure-centric environment, rather than a

Circle-of-Impact-aligned one, this fragmented way of looking at an organization results in the idea that it's just easier to treat everything, and everyone, as a functional part of the mechanism of the organization.

Let's return to our communication problem example. We know that customers are not responding to our communication. We send out informational brochures and emails, and post information on social media sites, trying to reach them with our message. What we don't see is that communication is a product of these three dimensions. Instead, we see ourselves locked away in our office, with the shades drawn, doors closed, yelling our message, hoping someone will hear. When they don't, we blame the client for not listening. To fix this problem, we need three qualities to surface into the life of the organization.

First, we need a clear reason why our communication with our customers is important. We need to be able to say what we expect the impact of our communication to be. What is it that we want them to do because of our communication with them? In this sense, the impact of communication is a change that takes place that is beneficial to both parties.

Second, we need to develop a relationship with our entire constituency—customers, employees, vendors, neighbors, and industry—so that they trust us. They need to believe that whatever we have to say is reflective of who we are as a company and is in their best interest as a member of our constituent community. Having developed a trusting relationship with them, we then know what their expectations are for our communication with them. We'll be communicating the kind of information they want, rather than just the information we have to distribute.

Third, we need to know the best method for communicating with them that accomplishes two goals. First, it strengthens their trust in us. Second, it lets them clearly know what kind of response that we would like them to make.

In the alignment that the Circle of Impact fosters, none of the three dimensions is more important than the other two. The three dimensions create a simple, practical way for us to work through the challenges that face us personally and in our businesses. In most situations, one of the dimensions appears to have the more critical need for change. While we begin with one of the dimensions, we bring the other two dimensions into the process to discover the solution that is always found in the alignment of the three dimensions.

Now in our communication situation, let's identify the problem area as a customer relationship that does not produce trust. The least-effective approach to resolving this problem is to go directly to the customer and tell them that we want to increase trust between us. Instead, we go directly to our customers asking them two simple questions: What kind of information do you need from us? And how would you like us to provide it to you? The solution that builds a trusting relationship is one where we listen and respond to them, rather than expecting them to respond to us.

A Network of Ideas

As I began to piece together the image of the Circle of Impact, I began to see a deeper reality unfolding. Certain values take prominence in organizational life. Integrity, efficiency, agility, alignment, and sustainability are some that have come to guide organizational leaders. The greater the clarity and practicality of these kinds of words, the stronger an organization can become. However, if you look at those words, they primarily represent conditions of the structural dimension of an organization.

I came to realize through working with leaders and their organizations that their problems were not just organizational. Within their teams and workforce, there were philosophical differences that made creating a culture of trust more difficult. I found that when the ideas that we identify as values were treated as secondary or optional aspects of the business, it also contributed to difficulties in how people worked together. Having trust in relationships is a product of clarity, of not just the *why* of the company, but the *how*. It doesn't take long talking with people from any business to discover if they are clear about the company's values and goals. When that clarity is missing, there is reticence on the part of employees to give their best each day.

The three dimensions of leadership of the Circle of Impact each have a simple goal for their practice. For the ideas dimension, it is clarity. Are people clear about the guiding values of the company? Is the company's purpose simple and practical? Does it describe the difference the company makes? Is there a clear understanding of the impact the company aims to achieve? By impact, I am speaking about the changes that make a difference that matters in the products or services that company produces, as well as how the company creates that impact in the marketplace. Finally, is there a clear sense of vision for how the whole of the company pursues the achievement of impact?

For the relationship dimension, the measure is trust. Is there a culture of respect in how people treat one another and how they are treated by the company? Trust is the product of a value culture of respect and integrity in the relational dimension. Trust is hard to build and easy to destroy. Is trust, therefore, a high priority for nourishment and sustainability?

For the structure dimension, the measure is agility, or the capacity for change within the context of constant transition. Agility is a commonly written about and discussed concept in business today. We, both our organizations and society on a global scale, are in the midst of a great transition. Organizations whose focus is preserving the legacy structure of their business will see change as an enemy and will not take the steps to develop their capacity for agility.

In the past, we'd take each dimension, and each of the words of our guiding ideology, and treat them separately. We'd have a values statement posted in the office. The company's purpose would be its brand. The company's vision would be a statement of *where* it wants to be in the future, and not about *how* we the people of the organization, working through the structure of the company, are going to achieve our goal for impact. And, lastly, over the course of two decades of consulting with organizations, I can count on one hand those who had a clear, compelling understanding of the impact or change that they wanted to bring to their customers and society at large. The perspective was never about change, but about how the company would benefit from growth.

The world of the fragmented organization is coming to an end. Increasingly, if you can't see how to integrate the whole of the business, then the business cannot compete. The Circle of Impact is a way of approaching the alignment of the company for impact. The other realization that I have had through this process of discovery is that you can't start big. You must start small, and the best place to start is individually. The following story is about a man who finds out that his life, career, and the life of his family is in transition. Here's how the Circle of Impact came to be used to help him become a person of impact.

A Career Transition Point: William's Story

William has worked for the same large corporation his whole career, first in sales and then for the past decade in management. The company is in the process of being acquired by a foreign company. William is pretty certain that his department and his job will be absorbed into the same office overseas. However, he isn't in a position to move his family overseas at this point in his career. For William and his family, this is a transition point in their lives. There is a moment of decision pressing in on them that will determine the course of their lives for the next decade or more.

William realizes that at his age and level of compensation, it is not easy to transfer to a new department or another company. He correctly sees himself at a transition point in his career. As he reflects on his situation with his wife and children, they decide that it is time to see what other opportunities are available to him outside the company. Does he start over in a new industry? Does he start his own business? His children will reach college age over the next few years, so financial considerations are important in this time of change.

I've seen many variations of this scenario over the years. I find that many people can tell you what they do and how well they do it, but they have a more difficult time saying what difference their work makes. Many people in William's situation often just jump into looking for the next job. They assume that the primary question before them is finding employment. However, like William, the more pertinent question concerns what they bring to a job. This is the moment of transition that William is in. He is confronted with a level of change that is unprecedented in his life. Before this moment, every change was logical, predictable, and incremental. Now it feels like he is crossing a threshold into a new land with an unknown frontier.

The Circle of Impact is not just helpful for a person like William who is at a mid-career transition. It is also true for any business that recognizes that it is also at a crossroads—a transition point—requiring change. Like William, we are all in transition. The context of our lives does not stay the same each year. Many people I talk to feel the pace of change is accelerating, and their capacity to absorb or respond to it is not adequate. Anxiety and fear of the unknown come to dominate their thinking about the future.

The Circle of Impact is a model that is not just for people and organizations going through change. It is, more importantly, how we can define our lives and the purpose of our organizations as creators of change that makes a difference that matters. A lot of people talk about being change agents and changing the world. However, when we come to a transition point, this is the time to move from talking about becoming a change leader to leading the change that makes a difference that matters.

As I saw this scenario played out in people's lives, I realized that it is insufficient just to plan our lives around what we do. We each do things every day related to work. Look at our calendars, filled with activities where we are doing things. Just doing things is not an adequate way to understand our lives, especially in a time of transition. For this reason, the principle of impact emerged in my understanding of what it means for us to live our best life. Define the impact that you want to have. Focus on it every day. Life becomes a bit simpler, as we can make choices as to what makes a difference and what doesn't. This is the transition point that William finds himself in.

Our Conversation

To apply the Circle of Impact to William's career transition, he begins by asking, *"What is the impact that I want to have?"* At this point, he doesn't know the answer. It is a question of purpose rising from the values that are important to him and his family.

William and I sit down for coffee and to discuss his situation. Our conversation goes like this:

"William, what has changed since you heard about the changes at work? How do you understand the transition point that you see yourself in the midst of right now?"

"As a family, we are choosing to see this change as an opportunity, not something to approach with fear. But in saying that, this is a very new experience for me, and I recognize that this is not like any decision that I have made before. I need some guidance and direction on how to think about this change."

From the perspective of the Circle of Impact at this point in the conversation, the transition point is specifically about the structure of William's work. However, the change that William is going through has more to do with his own self-perception than it does simply with where his next job comes from.

In our conversation, William admits that he has never really thought about his purpose. He realizes that he has absorbed the company's purpose as his own. He has been happy with the company because the company's values and his are well aligned. William's first step is to be able to see his life and work as something separate from the company. He needs to look at his life as a whole. He needs to see himself as a whole person—body, mind, and spirit—doing things that truly matter to him. He needs to understand his desire for meaning and significance that are expressions of his best self. And, he needs to see all this within the context of providing financially for his family. This is not a simple problem, with a simple solution. It is a complex one that needs a perspective that integrates all parts of his life.

"What is the impact that you have had over the years of working for your company? What changed because of who you are and what you did?"

These are questions related to the three dimensions of leadership. His answers describe more of the activities he did, the projects that were successful, and the growth in sales that he had early in his time with the company.

This is an experience many people have. They function as part of an organizational system without ever knowing the difference their work makes. Knowing one's impact is difficult to answer. It is not the same as producing results, though they are connected. It requires us to take the question to a deeper, more specific level of the Circle of Impact.

As William tells me his stories, and I follow up with more questions, he begins to see how his work made a difference. He develops a list of assets that characterize the value that he can bring to another organization. William can now say what he loved about his job, and why he was good at it. As a result, he begins to have a vision for the next chapter of his life.

Once he is clear about who he is, what his values and purpose for impact are, and the strengths that he brings to another work context, he can begin to bring the other two dimensions into the picture. William develops a short statement of what he has to offer an employer, and the impact that he wants to create. He develops a list of people whom he knows and trusts. Some he knows well, others only through friends. He goes to see each, and tells them his story, ending with this statement: *"Knowing now the impact that I want to create, who do you know that you think I should know? Will you connect us together?"* In this step, William is aligning his purpose of impact with people whom he trusts that can lead to another relationship within an organization where his values and strengths are assets that are needed.

For William, it now does not matter whether his next job is in a corporate office or with a small start-up business. What matters to him is being in a position to make a difference. Within a few weeks, an offer is made, he accepts, and William has successfully made the transition from where he was to where he will be in the future.

The Circle of Impact's Difference That Matters

Imagine having a clear sense of what you believe about yourself, being able to say with conviction, *"This is who I am and what my purpose for impact is."* From this perspective, we have something to offer an employer or a clear direction for the future. This is not simply a picture of our usefulness in life. It goes deeper than that. It is a picture of what motivates us to be at our best. It helps us to see ourselves functioning with impact in the social and work situations that we encounter every day. It helps us to know where we do not want to be.

For many of us, we have never thought of our lives or the work that we do in such terms. We have been led to think that we are parts of a system of production, just obediently or begrudgingly doing our job, until the whistle blows, and then we go home to do what we truly love doing. This separation of our personal life from our work life affects our perception of who we are. We don't see ourselves as whole persons. It is the same fragmented state experienced when the three dimensions of leadership are out of alignment. We find life confusing, our relationships conflicted, and the work we do unfulfilling.

Just as we want to create alignment of the three dimensions of leadership within our organizations, we also want this for our personal lives. We desire for our lives to be whole, complete in all that we do. We sort of see it, yet don't have the words to describe it. If we could put it to words, then we could do something about it. Until then, we are not sure how to cross over the threshold from self-doubt and fear, realizing that we are in the midst of a transition that we do not understand.

If you are at a point in your life and work where you sense a need for a change, then decide now to let reading this book become an opportunity to ask questions that can take you to a place where you find how your life matters. Do not settle just for an emotional belief that you have something to offer to the world. Instead, believe that what you have to offer matters in ways that you have never imagined. It is one thing to know *why* your life matters, which is your purpose for impact. It is a very different thing to know *how* your life matters. For when you bring the why of your life together with the how, you then can venture into those situations of transition with a confidence that you have something to offer and a way to bring change that makes a difference.

CHAPTER 1 QUESTIONS

The Circle of Impact—A Model for Leaders

1. What is the most pressing issue that you face right now? Are you at a transition point in your life and work? How would you describe this situation?

2. Is this issue an idea problem, a relationship problem, or a structure problem? Look to the other two dimensions for resources and solutions to bring an alignment to your situation.

3. What is the impact that you would like to have in the future? What is missing that you need to find to achieve the impact that you desire?

2

PERSONAL INITIATIVE FOR LEADERSHIP IMPACT

All leadership begins with personal initiative. This is a fundamental truth that I discovered as a program and organizational leader. I came to this view because I found myself caught between two competing perceptions of leadership. One is the idea that leadership is an organizational title and role. The other is that leadership is derived from the character of a person.

When I found myself failing in so many ways in my role as leader, yet still with the responsibility to perform at a high level of excellence, I knew something was broken. The pressure to be the do-it-all leader meant that my best talents would never have a chance to reach their potential, and that I would always be a captive to my limitations of ability.

It was here that I realized that the way organizations had come to be structured was the source of the problem. The obstacles that the structural design placed on people meant they, too, would never fulfill their potential with the company. In effect, businesses were alienating their most important asset by making it difficult for their people to take personal initiative to create impact that makes a difference that matters. This is a principal reason the Circle of Impact came into being.

Personal Initiative

When a person takes initiative, they make a personal choice to take action. It starts as motivation to fulfill a desire to fulfill the values that give their life meaning. It begins with an idea, leading to a decision, followed by a specific action. This change is the impact that is at the center of the Circle of Impact.

Three decades ago, when I was first introduced to the field of leadership, I quickly realized that my perspective on leadership was different from the conventional view. I did not see it as a role in an organization. Instead, it seemed clear to me that all leadership is a product of human action, whether by an individual or by a group. Leadership from this perspective is both personal and social. There is no limit to our capacity to lead, to make a difference, to resolve problems, to build bridges of communication, and to innovate new ways to function in organizations and society.

Take a moment to consider what I'm proposing here. I am saying that any person, no matter who they are or how ineffectual they may have been in the past, can take action that makes a difference that matters. It doesn't mean that we have to be perfect and highly talented, only that we are willing to take some initiative that produces a beneficial outcome.

It may seem that I am stating the obvious. Yes, of course anyone can do that. But not everyone *is* doing that. The range of obstacles that stand in the way of people taking leadership initiative can easily be identified when an organization's three dimensions of leadership are out of alignment. The following story is how one executive leader acted to elevate the leadership capacity of his division within his company.

When Personal Initiative Is Missing: Barry's Story

Marvin is a machine operator. Sam repairs and maintains the machine that Marvin works on every day. Ryan is their supervisor. Marvin and Sam have had an ongoing dispute about the condition and operation of the machine that Marvin uses. Marvin believes that Sam is not taking care of his machine as well as he should. Sam thinks Marvin is unreasonable, complaining to Ryan every time Marvin complains to him. After an initial try at a resolution, Ryan passes the problem up to his supervisor, who passes it along until it ends up on Barry's desk.

Barry is senior vice president at the company. He is frustrated. He talks about how frequently problems end up on his desk that should have been resolved at their point of origin. This practice of passing problems up the chain of authority has grown over the past decade. It has made his working relationship with the union more difficult. As problems are passed up the line, the situation transitions from being a problem, like that between Marvin and Sam, to being an issue between the company and the union. When it ends up on Barry's desk, it is no longer a problem to solve but an issue that requires negotiation.

How is it that this kind of problem persists in organizations? Barry concludes that this is a problem that began during a previous administration of the company. During that time, the executive suite made all the decisions. As a result, any personal initiative that a person like Marvin or Sam could make was discouraged. This is how Barry ends up spending a significant portion of each week putting out fires at the lowest level of the company.

Restructuring for Personal Initiative

The dispute between Marvin and Sam is symptomatic of a company where people are not free to solve problems. Rightly or wrongly, the perception that this sends to workers is that they cannot really be trusted to do the job that they are skilled and equipped to do. As this mindset becomes more deeply embedded in the attitudes and behaviors of employees, problems never get resolved, decreasing the efficiency and responsiveness of the company's workforce.

Barry decides to change this pattern of organizational behavior. He reasons that the problem is really a supervisory problem. Barry brings in a firm that specializes in organizational psychology to conduct training for Ryan and other managers like him. At the outset of the training, Barry introduces a new performance review system whose purpose is to monitor three areas that the training is addressing. He wants to see problems solved at the point of conflict. He wants to see more communication that bridges the boundaries of the company's structure. And he wants to see new ideas from people like Marvin and Sam tested and implemented.

With his new skills, Ryan negotiates an agreement with Marvin and Sam to create a process where issues between them can be resolved by them.

Five Steps to Get the Best from Your People

Whether you are a small business person or a corporate executive, getting the best work out of your people is one of the most challenging aspects of leadership. It takes more than attractive compensation packages and inspirational pep talks. It takes creating a culture of trust that unites people together around a common desire to give their best. Here are five steps any leader can take to build a relationship of trust with their team.

1. **Believe in them, so they will believe in themselves.** Every person that works for you has something to teach you. If you are open to learning from them they will gain the confidence to do their best work as partners with you.

2. **Free them to do their best work.** Don't micromanage them. To do so sends two messages: your lack of confidence in them and your lack of confidence in yourself. Remember, people can smell the fear in leaders and will respond accordingly. Be clear in expectations. Let them do it.

3. **Trust them.** Trust is hard to win, easy to lose. Trust everyone until you have a real reason not to. Be constant and consistent in trusting them. Train and supervise with trust in mind and a culture of trust will grow.

4. **Thank them personally.** Gratitude is not a reward. It is appreciation. It is hard to be grateful if you don't know employees personally, by name, and what their work for the company is. Gratitude has its greatest impact when it is least expected. Making it personal makes it real.

5. **Honor them.** This is partly gratitude but it's more the way you treat both individuals and teams with dignity and respect. Remember, *they don't work for you*, they work for your customers. *You work for them* to create an environment of belief, freedom, trust, and gratitude that enables them to do their best work. This is what leaders do.

Why Personal Initiative Matters

To make a difference that matters does not have to be a big project or the creation of a business. All that is required is for a person to act upon the values that are important to them. It can be a simple comment while standing on a street corner. It can be an act of kindness, an expression of gratitude, or a display of courage. It can be a word of honesty in a meeting or an act of sacrifice to help a friend in need. It just has to be an act of personal initiative that creates a change that matters.

Leadership begins with personal initiative because, increasingly, companies depend upon their people taking steps to do the right thing in the moment of need. In the past, when we defined leadership as a title or a role, we were saying that organizational structure was the defining characteristic of leadership. The result was that anyone below the level of CEO could essentially say, "That's not my job" and pass it up to their supervisor or manager.

Small problems became large issues because initiative was squeezed out of the system. Maintaining order and integrity in the system of operation became the purpose of the company. The result was the spread of organizational silos that compartmentalized the legacy structures of the past.

The speed of change that impacts us today requires organizations to be agile and adaptive in responding to changing circumstances. It isn't just that organizations need leaders who are equipped to take personal action within the parameters of the values and purpose of the organization. We need it through all kinds of institutional settings in society. Everyone, regardless of who they are, where they are from, or what their educational and occupational credentials are, need to be practicing leadership initiative.

When leadership is understood as a function of human initiative, then the motivation to take initiative is a personal one. The supervision of employees cannot simply be based upon an employment contract. Rather, the leadership initiative of employees needs to be encouraged as essential to the health and vitality of the company.

To say that we want people to take personal initiative is not to say that any initiative is okay. Rather, we need people to operate within a culture of shared values that guide the company, and therefore guide the decisions and actions of every individual. Simply advocating for great employees to have greater responsibility will not work without an alignment of the three dimensions of leadership of the Circle of Impact.

The Path from Personal Initiative
to Leadership Impact

Personal initiative becomes leadership impact when our actions influence others to act with us in a shared, coordinated fashion. This is the key to understanding leadership in the 21st century. It is both personal and social.

As a consultant for two decades, I had conversations every day about what it was like to work in a business or a nonprofit organization. Just by listening, by asking respectful questions, people will tell you about their experiences. I was always fascinated to discover how negative people's experiences at work were. The most common complaint was that the way things were organized made work harder, not easier. They would speak about ways that things could be different. I'd silently think, *"I wonder what percentage of her potential she is reaching at work?"*

Our potential is not a defined amount of good that we can produce in our jobs or lives. There is no box out of which we draw our defined amount of life potential. Rather, potential is the opportunity that comes from an environment of openness to create impact, which is released through personal initiative.

Many of us seek to live quiet, respectable lives of meaning and service to people and places we care about. Too often, we find that we are bound by the obstacles that society and organizational structure place before us that keep us from realizing our potential. Most of us never even think that we have potential. Do you want to know your potential? State what you care about, and how things would be different if you could give your whole self to its betterment. Remove the obstacles and watch what happens.

These obstacles to fulfilling our potential occur because we allow ourselves to be defined by social and organizational situations that have no clear purpose or outlet for creating impact.

Yet down deep within us are desires that constantly suggest to us that we are made for more than what we are doing. People join projects of participatory philanthropy, like breast cancer walks, or work at a soup kitchen for the poor and homeless, because they desire to live lives that matter beyond the mundane exercise of their daily duties. They spend their days sitting in offices looking forward to taking personal initiative outside of work. As a result, the potential for people to make a difference that matters at work is not even considered.

The path from personal initiative to leadership impact is achieved by removing obstacles of the mind, body, and spirit where our desires find their expression. Obstacles of small ambition. Obstacles of poor discipline in how we live. Obstacles of relationships that we allow to hold us back from believing that if we give ourselves to some desire to make a difference, then we can achieve our goal. These are personal obstacles that we can change.

There are also the organizational obstacles of structure and institutional purpose, which treat people as cogs in a production machine. As long as a company functions this way, the people with a desire to make a difference that matters will decide to go someplace else. Retention of good people is achieved by creating a culture of values that support personal initiative.

Our desire to make a difference that matters erupts from time to time in a moment of opportunity. These feelings are a signal to us about our potential legacy. Think of your life as a story that will be told by the generations that follow you. Your story is not about the results, but about the character of your life. At this point, all this may sound absurd. If it does, you have then identified one of the obstacles that stands in the way of reaching your life's potential.

There is no limit to our potential. But it does not mean that we can just go do anything. It means that our potential for impact is greater than our imagination can visualize. It is true today. It will be true on the last day of our time on this earth.

Consider the following questions:

"Do I want a life where I can make a difference on an ever-ascending scale of significance? Or do I want to live a quiet life focused on satisfying my own interests?"

"What is that thing within me—a belief or a feeling, my passion—that is so important, so powerful a force that I can no longer ignore it and be happy?"

This is your motivation to make a difference that matters. It is that deep desire that is calling you to step out of your place of comfort and security, to take some creative action to make a difference that matters. It is calling you to follow your potential impact as a person.

If you are an executive in a business, this is the kind of leadership impact you want from your people. The potential benefit to a company grows each time personal initiative that matters is taken. Remove the obstacles to people working together, innovating, and solving the immediate problems of their work situation, and you open the possibilities for growth and strength that were locked away in the people of the organization. However, for this shift in perception of our human potential to work for the people in your business, it must begin with you. Your own self-perception as a person taking leadership initiative is where you must begin. Your change of perception will lead the way for others to follow in joining you to create a leadership-rich organization.

Impact is a change that makes a difference that matters. It is a wise word when no word was expected. It is the identification with a family's suffering at the loss of a child that creates a shared community of grief that begins the healing. It is the refusal to let declining results demoralize a team. It is a belief expressed in action that the past doesn't define the future.

Impact is not business as usual. It is the line operator saying, *"Stop! This is not working."* It is the supervisor respecting the line operator by listening, and in collaboration with all those touched by this line operator's initiative, fixing the problem. It is the CEO going to the line to personally thank the line operator for his leadership.

Impact is not the system working as it always has, but just a little better. It is changing the system so that each part can reach its potential.

Impact isn't just about fixing problems or working for better communication or figuring out new ways to do what has been accepted as tried and true. Rather, it is going to the root and foundation of everything about us as persons, and the institutions and organizations where we spend our lives, and asking the questions, *"What difference do I make? What difference does this product make to the customer? What difference does this business make to our community?"* Then, we can solve our problems, communicate better, and create innovative ways to work.

In talking about creating impact, we are talking about a cultural change. The traditional measures of profit and loss, market share, and growth-over-time are still relevant. In addition, we ask, what is the impact of those numbers upon our perception of the impact that we are creating as a company?

The change context begins with our perception of what the impact of our lives and the work of our companies is. Imagine that you are flying across the country. You have three to four hours with the person in the seat next to you. Taxiing out to the runway, she asks what you do. You could tell her exactly what you do. Talk on the phone, fill out forms, answer email, sit in meetings. Or you could describe to her how your insurance agency is different. You tell her of your focus on serving your customers. In telling her that story, you are telling her of the impact that your company is creating in the marketplace.

In the Circle of Impact model, impact stands above everything else. It is the ultimate measure of our ideas, our values, our purpose, our relationships, the social and organizational structures of our businesses, our society, and in the end, what defines our legacy. Everything else is commentary that just shows us how much alike we are to everyone else.

Impact is why things fall apart, why they hold together when they shouldn't, and is the impetus for all that we love and hope for in the world. It is why we invest in people, businesses, communities, and ourselves. When we know something is not quite right, we don't settle for things to remain the same. We take initiative to change it. The result of our initiative is the impact which makes a difference that matters.

CHAPTER 2 QUESTIONS

Personal Initiative for Leadership Impact

1. If I could change one thing, anything in the world, right now, what would it be? Why this one thing?

2. If I were to take personal initiative every day to make a difference that matters, what would I do today?

3. Who has taken personal initiative to make a difference in my life? Thank them before the next time the sun sets.

3

BECOMING A CIRCLE OF IMPACT LEADER

Circle of Impact is a model of leadership focused on the creation of impact by people and their organizations. Impact is a change that occurs because of the personal initiative that is taken. The difference compared to conventional organization-based leadership models is that a manager or a machine operator can both function as leaders within the context of their work. Circle of Impact's ultimate purpose is to equip each member of an organization with the values, skills, and freedom to take personal initiative to improve performance.

If all leadership begins with personal initiative, then all leadership is personal. By personal, I mean it is the individual, regardless of who they are, acting upon their own sense of what needs to be done within the context of the situation that they are in. It does not mean that everyone can do anything they want. It means they act according to their own sense of identity and purpose within the role that they serve. The difference is that they are free to act to create the impact that is needed.

For example, when a person's simple act of sacrifice saves a child from a burning car, but she loses her own life, she is a Circle of Impact Leader. Deciding, in that moment, to walk towards the burning car, instead of standing by and watching it burn, we are seeing the deep values that define this person. Tragic, yes. Yet, for the child and the child's family, her act of sacrificial leadership is transformational.

When a line manager stops the line, even in the face of missing daily quotas, to bring the quality measures back into alignment, he is acting as a Circle of Impact Leader. It is not the action that defines us, but the impact of the action that defines us.

When a young girl starts a website to share stories of courage by girls and boys who are doing things in their local schools and neighborhoods to counteract bullying, she is a Circle of Impact Leader.

When a tourist, having traveled to a vacation spot far from home, is touched by the poverty of the children that he meets, he returns home to start a charity to improve the schools of these children. He is acting as a Circle of Impact Leader.

None of these people were asked to take the action that they did. They responded to the situation out of their own sense of identity reflected in their values. To take initiative to change the course of a person's life, even if it costs their own life, is a true measure of leadership. People acknowledge the heroism of the act. At the same time, they think, I'm not like that person. That is correct. None of us may be like her. Are we supposed to be? Maybe we are, but only as it is a reflection of our true selves. Within us are desires that point us to the kinds of actions that are indicative of who we are, of what matters to us, and how we want our lives to be experienced. You may not sacrifice your life for another person. But you can give yourself to something you believe in.

Most leadership is not heroic. What is heroic gets the attention because it is exceptional, not the norm for most of us. Circle of Impact Leadership is not foremost about drawing attention to yourself. It is about the impact that we seek. We want to create some beneficial change in some specific place that is important to us. Our simple, practical acts of initiative are personal because the people, the organization, or the community where it takes place matters to us.

An act of Circle of Impact Leadership may be a small, mostly hidden decision to spend three minutes more with a patient, listening to what they feel is important for their physician to know, rather than quickly leaving the room. She takes this action because her relationship with the patient matters to her. The patient is not just an appointment on her calendar. The patient is a real person for whom she provides more than technical medical care.

Whether the initiative is heroic or quiet, Circle of Impact Leadership begins with the understanding that leadership is a deep personal expression, revealing our potential for impact, and leading us to understand who our best selves can be.

The Personal and the Social

Circle of Impact Leadership, as a very personal experience, is not a job, but an expression of the values that matter to us. People don't aspire to lead without a reason that moves them to make the sacrifices, to do the hard work, and stay committed for years. Leadership touches the full range of what it means to be a human being. Taking personal initiative to make a difference that matters can take place in any setting. Whether at work, at home, in our community, or online, we can act to create impact. Every one of us is born with this capacity to lead. The ways we make a difference may differ among us, but the act of taking personal initiative is the same for us all. From this perspective it is important that we see that Circle of Impact Leadership is both personal and social.

Listen to the stories that people share about their lives. There is always a relationship at the center of it. The person inspired us as our mentor. Or the verbal abuse we received from our supervisor finally got us mad enough to stand up for ourselves. Our acts of leadership don't happen in a vacuum. They occur in the midst of the daily living of our lives.

The social dimension is where the personal takes place. We do things for people. We are influenced by people we look to as leaders. We mobilize our team to take on an important challenge. The vast majority of our actions are focused on changing some aspect of the relationship that we have with people. This has always been the true nature of leadership. It may be personal, but the personal always takes place within a social environment.

The Identity of a Circle of Impact Leader

The joining of the personal with the social is where we find our lives. We need to know who we are. We can't really know except in the context of our relationships with people. It is really our first step beyond ourselves where we can experience a world that is greater than what our mind can conceive. When we can do that, we can begin to see that our lives can have a far greater impact than what we have imagined up to this point.

This idea that relationships are at the center of the way the world works is not just a practical idea. It serves as an organizing principle for our lives. If we ask, *"What is my relationship to this person, this group, this community, this natural environment?"* we begin to see why these connections matter to us. Understanding this connection tells us something about ourselves. Our identity begins to take shape when we decide what matters to us, and what doesn't.

Some of my friends and family are ocean lovers. They will go to the beach every opportunity that they can. Some of them go beyond loving it for recreational and vacation purposes. They are committed to the health and welfare of the oceans. They invest time and money in their love for the sea.

I feel the same way about the mountains. I live in the mountains of Wyoming. There is something deep and resonant about these "hills of Wyoming" that feed my sense of wholeness and connection to the natural world. Our sense of identity as individuals is directly related to our relationships with one another and the places we live and work.

My family has had an indelible impact upon my sense of who I am. My desire to understand the world, for friendship, and to have my life make a difference, is all derived from the way I was raised. The values of freedom and responsibility, connection to my family's past, and the grace and forgiveness constantly shown to me by my parents, were just the way we lived. Except for one statement that my grandmother made to me as a young adolescent, I do not recall there ever being any kind of declaration of our values. No list. No manifesto of our family's values. We were simply told family stories that had a practical point that we shouldn't miss. The comment that my grandmother made to me, which has stayed with me ever since, was, "Whatever you do, do not bring shame to the family name." Her words gave me boundaries for the freedom that I have felt to pursue my interests and ambition.

I recognize that my experience is increasingly atypical. Families have become less a place of nurture and more a place for social positioning. Children are prepped to fill a role in society. There is a paralyzing pressure to conform to the social expectations that govern society. Online websites and bookstores are full of material encouraging us to be our true self and discover our true calling. This is a good thing. Except that, for many people, the social and organizational structures that we need to nurture our sense of self are missing. All we know then is the pressure to conform without the opportunity to find our true selves.

Bowing to this social pressure to conform ultimately means that we lose a part of our selves. The social obligation to conform doesn't liberate us to find our true selves. Uncertainty and insecurity grow because we have no clear sense about what our future lives should be like. To discover our true selves, we need to have a clear sense of our personal identity and how we function within the wide range of social situations we experience daily. From this, our self-confidence grows, and from it, the actions of initiative which made a difference to the people and places that matter to us.

Part of the transition that our world is going through is that the homogeneous social structures that marked earlier decades, which made it easier to establish ourselves in a social setting, to fit in, to find our place in the world, are no longer as they once were. Today our culture is fragmented into narrowly conceived tribal enclaves that have little room for being an individual and fitting in at the same time. This social transition will continue as new kinds of groups form around a shared desire for impact.

I see this in particular in communities where natural tragedies have devastated people's lives, homes, and business. The way the citizens of their communities come together to help their neighbors is evidence to me that social unity can be born out of the individual personal initiative to do something that helps those impacted.

Circle of Impact Leaders are not conformists. They are initiators. They create new and good effects for families, their organizations, and their communities. They selflessly act from their own clear sense of who they are. They claim a freedom for their lives that frees them from fear, doubt, and confusion. They gain confidence, perspective, and humility as they embrace the complexity of the world that we are transitioning into.

Every person that I meet and connect with on a personal level has the potential to live a life that makes a difference that matters. Every single one. Too often, the story they tell me of their lives is someone else's story for them. Their stories have a flatness to them. There is a lack of passion or a boredom that I hear in their voice. This is what happens when conformity has replaced taking personal initiative to create impact. These people have yet to discover their true selves.

Then there are those who have a unique story to tell. For some, as they tell their story, they begin to see something that was missing before. They begin to visualize the fulfillment of their potential. It is not unusual, then, to begin to talk about how they can start over. I had this conversation that has led to the writing of this book, the beginning of a new business and life in a new community. I recognize that I am not the first in my family to do this. My grandfather and my great-great-grandfather both quit the businesses they were in to volunteer to go to war. Afterwards they did not return to their previous careers but ventured off into new ones. This is the sort of thing that happens to people when they begin to see the practical implications of their potential for impact.

The desire to be our true selves is a good thing. We should read books, listen to podcasts, hire coaches, and develop new skills to create our capacity for having an impact. We cannot know fully our potential for impact until we begin to take action. When we start taking initiative, beginning with small steps and growing bigger as we learn, we see what is possible to be accomplished in our life. If there is nothing else you get from reading *Circle of Impact*, I wish that you can visualize the full potential that your life has for making a difference in your world. Then you have a grasp on the meaning and significance that your life can have when you discover your true self.

Is there a passion calling you to take initiative to do something? Let your passion guide you. As you take steps forward, continually ask, *"What is the impact that I want in this situation? What is the change that I can create?"* Never stop asking these questions. Never settle for half measures or easy answers. Never settle for the flat conformity of fitting in. Practice taking initiative to make a difference, and you will quickly become a person of impact, a genuine Circle of Impact Leader.

A Future for Leadership

Circle of Impact Leadership is the future of leadership in organizations and society. It represents a significant reorientation in how we see and practice leadership. There has always been a facet of leadership practice, hidden from view, of the person of impact. Here the character of a person exhibited in their acts of initiative is a leading indicator of the future of leadership. It is personally expressed through social relationships in organizations and communities. In the past, leadership was viewed as the influence of the *"leaders"* of organizations setting an example for others to follow. Circle of Impact Leadership is a shift of focus to the creation of impact. Influence has value only to the extent that it creates change in the perceptions and actions of people to make a difference that matters.

The shift to an impact focus means that each member is being freed to take personal initiative to solve problems and create new strengths for the company. This means that how people are supervised, how they are trained, how they are supported requires strategic shift in perception and design of the company. This transformation means that the organization becomes a leader-rich company. A culture of trust, ambition, and collaboration emerges that energizes the company as it experiences the transition that is taking place in the world.

The future of organizations demands a different leadership approach to its organization. As automation replaces repetitive skilled jobs, the people who remain in the business become more important to the success of the company. They are being asked to do more. They are expected to take greater personal

41

responsibility for the impact of their work. They need to be able to see the value of their contribution to the company. When they are equipped to be Circle of Impact Leaders, the company becomes more agile and aligned for impact. Then the organization can become a Circle of Impact company.

Aligning for Leadership

If we look at leadership through the lens of the three dimensions of leadership of the Circle of Impact, we can see how a fragmented kind of leadership has been a normal arrangement in organizations.

An ideas-centric understanding of leadership focuses on the psychology and philosophy of leading. Biographies of historic leaders explore styles, traits, and strategies for leadership. Social scientists study organizational leadership to better understand its phenomenon. Academic researchers provide insight into best practices for building teams, leading change, and functioning as senior executives. Yet ideas remain ideas. The strategic value does not have an effective structure for impact.

A relational-centric understanding of leadership focuses on the place of influence in motivating people to work better together. The social aspects of team leadership are addressed for building cultures of trust and collaboration. These cultures are vital for improving team functioning, a good thing for any organization. When improved relationships are seen as a tactical exercise to resolve internal conflicts, then the potential that resides in greater trust and cooperation may never be realized. For the company, it is important to ask whether relationships have a strategic role to play.

A structure-centric understanding of leadership is what most organizations have. The strategic focus is on the management of the parts of the system of organization. In general, those aspects are products or services, operations, finance, and governance. Each has their prescribed system of measurement. The Circle of Impact Leadership question to ask of each is, *"What is the desired impact and how is that change measured?"*

My observation is that if an alignment of the three dimensions is not achieved, the structure-centric becomes the default perspective. With that comes resistance to change, less clarity about values and purpose, and more difficulty creating a culture of trust. With those dimensions missing or diminished, it is difficult to create an increasingly agile company.

Circle of Impact alignment is created by each dimension equally working together to create the conditions for impact. We come to understand the impact that we want by asking questions that get at the change that needs to happen for those the organization serves. Alignment is impact-centric focused on creating a change that matters. It addresses the real issues of system integration in organizations. Leadership for alignment begins at the top and engages the whole of the company in the conversation that leads to a commitment to becoming an impact-centric organization. The Circle of Impact is a model to get to that point.

The way we get to alignment is by asking questions that continue to focus us on the change we want to create. Impact is a particular organizational outcome whose perspective has been missing in virtually every organization that I have worked with over the past four decades. Few people can answer, *"What is the impact of your organization? What is the change that you want to create?"*

In a structure-centric organization, the question of impact challenges the system to explain how improving operational efficiency creates a desired impact. In a relationship-centric organization, the question of impact challenges the notion that creating a culture of trust is a primary end result. In an ideas-centric organization, the question of impact challenges the notion that a clear and logical plan is the aim of the business.

The question of impact for a Circle of Impact Leader is a simple one. What is it that you want to change? What changes do you need to make to achieve your goal?

This is a reorientation of the way we think about our role in organizations. Roles are task- and activity-oriented. Just because every minute of every work day is scheduled does not mean that we have been effective. We may be highly ineffective because our calendar reflects a system of putting out fires, rather than one that creates impact. The leadership of personal initiative is impact-oriented. A company of Circle of Impact Leaders is a company that no longer has to pull everyone along to get minimum results. It is a company that is in sync and aligned for each person doing what they must to create the impact that defines the business.

I often ask people, *"At the end of your life, what do you want your legacy to be?"* No one ever speaks about their impact. No one ever speaks about their activity schedule. They usually say something about how people remember them as a success, a good guy, or a dependable worker. It is rarely clear and definitive. This is a mark of the transition that our world is in. If we can't, each of us, say this is how I want my life and work, my company, my family, my community, to be different in a week, a year, three years, at the end of our life, then we have an alignment problem. We are not aligned to lead a life where our true selves flourish.

We live in a leader-starved society. We don't need more leaders who inhabit the title of leader in a business. We need more people who will step forward to become Circle of Impact Leaders within the business. When they do, then we discover the full potential for impact that will be the mark of leadership in the future.

CHAPTER 3 QUESTIONS

Becoming a Circle of Impact Leader

1. What is the one thing about which you feel more positive passion than anything else? Why is this important? What is its impact upon you and your life?

2. If you could change one thing connected to your passion, anything within your power to change, what would it be? Once you changed it, what would you say is the impact that you have had?

3. Do you desire to be a Circle of Impact Leader? If you would take personal initiative to create the change that you desire in Question #2, you would have taken your first step towards becoming a person of impact.

PART TWO

WE ARE ALL IN TRANSITION

④

LEADERSHIP
IN TRANSITION

"*A*re you a leader?*" I often ask people this question. I want to know if they see themselves as leaders. When I first began to ask this question more than two decades ago, I was surprised by the pushback that I got. My assumption was that people would be complimented by my question. They weren't. Most of the time people said no. Their response wasn't a nice sort of humble deflection of a compliment. Instead, I felt that I had offended them. This did not make sense to me.

I would then dig a little deeper and ask why. Almost universally their response would be either *"I don't want to be the boss"* or *"I don't want all that responsibility."* They saw leadership as setting a person apart for responsibility and recognition. In their view, leaders have a target on their back. It is a position of vulnerability and exposure to scrutiny that they didn't want. Many times, they told me of ruined friendships because one of their colleagues became their boss. Don't call them a leader because it means isolation and pain.

Leadership is a kind of universal term that represents some kind of superlative. *"She's a leader in her field." "He's a thought leader." "We are the industry leader in…"* Leadership isn't an object. You can't go buy it online. We see it as a title or an organizational role. Yet it comes out awkwardly if we say, "I work for Leader Jones." It isn't a thing, but a quality that we use to describe someone or something.

Our Perception of Leadership

The most basic, universal use of the word *"leader"* is to distinguish a person from those who are followers. This is not how I am using the word. *Why is this person designated as a leader and that person a follower? Is it the role within an organization or a particular social structure that they have?*

Think about the teams that you are on. To achieve your goals, each of you performs as a leader and a follower as necessary. On teams, and in other collaborative environments, we need the skills and the mindset to be both, sometimes at the same time. The old hierarchical structure of organizations assumed that there was one leader. Whomever was in charge was the leader. Everyone else was a follower. Leadership, from this 20th-century perspective, was about top-down delegation of work. Those days of leadership are fading quickly. The technical sophistication of organizational life and the pace of change mean that no one person has all the knowledge or expertise to be the sole leader. Leadership is quickly shifting from an organizational role that a person is assigned to perform to the function of people within the role that they have. Character and creativity are marks of leadership that each person within an organization can now demonstrate.

Leadership in Transition

There is a simple explanation as to how we came to view leadership as an organizational role. Our perception is based on how organizations have been structured. With the emergence of the modern industrial organization, the roles of people changed. In the past, they may have been shopkeepers, farmers, teachers, or clerks in an office. The advent of the factory assembly line meant that work was delegated, regulated, and repetitive. A new economic class of middle-class managers emerged. The social dimension of work became what happened during breaks or after work. This was a transformational change in how society functioned. Now a new transition is taking place, from the mass production assembly line to customized manufacturing on a global scale.

I saw this transition firsthand in a change project for a textile company. The 17-step process for making socks was broken. Each step existed as a separate process, disconnected from the one before and the one after. The people who worked each step were trained only for that one step. Their job each day was to do their assigned task for eight hours. No cross-training. No integration of the process to produce efficiency and possibilities for growth. No consideration for inventory control, as each step generated its own level. Our project's purpose was to integrate the process. As a result, the time for making a pair of men's dress socks was reduced from six weeks to six days.

We have spent, as a society, a millennium or more with a view that there are bosses and workers, leaders and followers. Our job is to follow. This experience is now changing. In the future, companies will become leader-rich organizations because the complexity and scale of change that is happening requires more people to take a greater responsibility for the outcome of the business' operation.

People are human beings who by their very nature are creative and social. When organizational leaders began to realize this, they started talking about followership as a component of leadership, a positive step forward in understanding the value of people in an organization. Yet even from this perspective, leadership is still defined as a role within the structure of the modern organization. In effect, where you fit in the hierarchy defines your value to the organization.

The cultural dominance of the hierarchical model remains with us. It influences how we view the world at large. It is a difficult perception to change. It is why people still push back when I ask the question, *"Are you a leader?"*

Where Leadership Starts

All leadership begins with personal initiative. It is an act of personal choice. We choose to do something. We choose not to do it. The choice leads to a change. Not just any change, but one that is intentional and purposeful.

Leadership is open to anyone. It does not discriminate. All that is required is a person taking initiative to make a difference. This is the sole basis of what it means to be a leader from the perspective of the Circle of Impact. All leadership begins with personal initiative to create impact that makes a difference that matters. This is all that it takes to lead.

The former way of understanding leadership is complex. As a follower, we operate with a limited understanding of the leader's intentions and organizational context. We were removed from an immediate and intimate relationship to the leader. Fear, doubt, and a lack of trust are normal aspects of relating to leaders in this way that is now in transition.

Circle of Impact Leadership is rather simple. Too simple? I don't think so. It is also practical. Too practical? How can that be? Just decide what is important, then act to make a difference that matters.

Imagine how you spend each day. In your mind, walk through a typical day, from the moment of waking up through work, time with family and friends, then into the evening and rest. Can you see how each moment you are presented with opportunities filled with purposeful acts of impact? The moment you see the solution to a client's dilemma, you make the call. Unexpected, yet deeply appreciated, you make a difference for them. The moment in conversation with your assistant you say, "Tell me which way will make it easier for you to get this done." The look on his face tells you that you have relieved him of the fear of the project not being on time and over budget. The moment you decide to turn team meetings over to the team to design and carry out you see what you didn't before, that the meetings are not about you, but them. Can you see the difference that your life can have? Imagine every day like this. More importantly, can you imagine your team and your family operating with this mindset?

Really, Anyone Can Be a Leader

Taking leadership initiative doesn't mean that everyone becomes a CEO. Rather, it means that everyone becomes a high-level contributor of impact. Leadership is not the role or the title, but how we function within the context of our lives. It is not limited to work. It involves every aspect of our lives.

I first saw this principle at work at the college where I served. I was the college's chaplain and director of leadership programs. Along with the other offices on campus that served students outside the classroom, we were always trying to understand what was happening with students. One semester, we conducted a survey to discover which members of the staff had the most one-to-one contact with students. No, it wasn't faculty, nor the athletic coaches. It was not even the student affairs staff. It was the housekeeping staff in the residence halls. These almost-invisible members of the college community had daily interaction with students. They were in a unique position to see the ups-and-downs of students' lives. As a result, we invited them to join our team. We met regularly with them to talk about what they saw, and how they could support the students.

When I ask people if they are leaders, and they reject the idea, I then ask them about the things that they do that make a difference in the lives of people and their communities. They tell me stories of the places they serve, the people that they help, and the contributions that they are making in their communities. They may not want to be the boss or desire to have the responsibilities of a CEO but they are functioning as leaders nonetheless. They are making decisions to act to make a difference that matters.

They lead in all kinds of ways. They serve on community boards. They help build Habitat for Humanity homes for low-income families. They coach youth sports teams. They deliver meals to homebound seniors. They write music, sing in choirs, and perform in community theater. They are painters, jewelry designers, and writers of poetry. They run for public office. They mentor underprivileged children in reading and math. For many their genuine contribution as leaders happens outside of their job. They, too, are invisible, except to those whose lives are changed by their acts of leadership initiative.

Many people are contributing leadership at work. They serve on company task forces, help coworkers meet deadlines, and offer words of encouragement to clerical staff. They solve problems, collaborate across departmental boundaries. They take continuing education courses to improve their knowledge and skills. They innovate ways of improving processes that are no longer as effective. They listen and support coworkers who are struggling with problems at home. They share ideas to help others. They contribute as high-performing team members. Leadership is happening. It is just not happening as a function of the role, but rather as an expression of the character of the person.

Each one of those activities begins with a decision by the individual to do something rather than nothing. They step into action because they want to make a difference right here, right now. Leadership is an active expression of a person's values. We know who they are by what they do. They are leaders because they show us what matters to them by their actions. Passivity is not a leadership quality. Action is. Leaders lead through their actions, even when the action is not to take action. As leaders, we need to connect to *why* taking this action is important to us personally.

The Why of Personal Initiative

A person who takes initiative is doing it for a reason. Genuine leadership is personal. It rises from within us. It is motivated by our desire for personal meaning, for happy, healthy relationships and for making a difference that matters. The initiative could be a small act of kindness like holding a door open for someone whose arms are filled with packages. Or it could be something large, like the formation of a health organization to eradicate a tropical disease in a developing country. The measure of leadership is defined by the impact that comes from our purpose for making a difference.

In acts of personal initiative, we see individual statements of purpose expressed. We better understand people by observing how they act. When their words align with their actions, then we have a more complete picture of who this person is. Acts of purpose reveal to us the values that define the person.

When Margaret, the office receptionist, brings fresh flowers every week for the reception area, she does so because she believes that it matters. To her if one person a day goes over and smells the flowers, she knows she has made their day a bit brighter. It is a small act that makes a difference. In the world of business, every day is filled with small acts that are intended to make a difference. This is how leadership is born out of personal initiative.

The action may be so representative of the attitude and behavior of the person that no one thinks of it as an act of leadership. They say, *"That is Margaret being Margaret."* If Margaret retires or misses work for a few weeks because of illness, her absence is noticed because the flowers that she brings each week are not there. These small acts of leadership are often taken for granted. We, therefore, need to take the personal initiative to recognize these moments of impact with gratitude.

Leadership is a personal expression of our values and purpose. It is also a social one. Margaret acts out of her desire to bring beauty to the office each week. She does this as a personal expression of her desire to make a difference. While the act is worthy of our thanks, the measure of impact is a question of change.

Margaret's act of bringing beauty into the office touches the lives of guests to the office. However, her act would be more easily seen as an act of leadership if other people began to do things to change the atmosphere of the office. The measure of leadership is not the act itself, but the impact that is created. Margaret's act is what I call a *"start small, grow big"* one. It is a small act to bring flowers each week. It makes a small difference. But it is not a sustainable one if her act of initiative has not become a socially shared one. If Margaret's purpose is just personal, then her act of impact upon the office may well fade once she is no longer employed there. If, however, the other staff's response to Margaret's weekly gift of kindness to the office is to begin to look for other ways to improve the office's environment, then her small act of leadership has provided the motivation for others to join her in leadership. Margaret's example to the staff is her freedom to make a difference. As a result, the office staff begins to take initiative to improve how they work together and how clients find the office a comfortable place to conduct business. In this, Margaret has inspired leadership initiative.

Leadership is both personal and social. The measure of leadership is not the act itself, but the impact that comes from the act. Circle of Impact Leadership is more than personal. It is social because it is through the social that sustainable impact is found. Without the social, the personal can be self-serving. Without the personal, the social can miss the larger opportunity to create a change that matters.

The Real Transition in Leadership

What I have described here is really not new. People have been taking initiative to make a difference that matters since the first human community formed. This is how we live together. We share our lives through acts of service and shared work. What is different is that I am saying that this is where leadership begins. It begins in the hearts and minds of people who want a better world than the one they experience now.

The real transition in leadership is a change in perception of its place within organizations. The emergence of digital technology over the past four decades has changed how we work in organizations. Technological innovation has impacted us as individuals in two specific ways.

Each of us now has access to a wider range of knowledge than ever before. Using our handheld devices, we can type in a phrase and find out information in a few moments that less than two generations ago was only available from a large university research center. The possibility for translating all this new knowledge into world-changing impact is virtually limitless. All it takes is the desire to make a difference and the will to work hard to make it happen. It does not mean that success will come to everyone in the same way. It does mean that the tools and information are at hand for anyone to create impact.

This technological change also means that the barriers that once stood in a person's way to do things that make a difference are disappearing. Networks are an emerging type of organizational structure where our relationships with one another matter more than ever. Now we can be a part of a growing social context where the value of human interaction matters. With that same handheld device, one person working in an office can contact a person, met through social media, living a dozen time zones away, to ask a question or seek opportunities for collaboration. This is not the future promise of the digital age; it is a reality now.

This transition in leadership is also a social one. Technology can serve us in our interactions with one another if we are intentional in doing so. The social implications for our ability to collaborate with one another regardless of who we are and where we live mean that the context of leadership is changing. It is shifting from a role defined by our job description to one where we are taking personal initiative in concert with other people. The limitations of legacy organizational structures are becoming more significant. The future in this regard is a social one, where our networks of relationships grow to create new opportunities for impact.

This new way of understanding leadership is in its very beginning stages. The first stage of change is in our self-perception. We must see that the actions we take to create impact are leadership ones. The second stage is to see that our leadership initiatives happen in our relationships with people with who we daily interact, like our families, the people in our businesses, and local community. As we learn to live in this new leadership reality, we grow from a local orientation to see how our impact can happen on a global scale. Two principles guide this transition to ensure that it remains simple and practical. We need to "Start Small in Order to Grow Big." And, we need to "Act Locally on a Global Scale" by sharing our stories of leadership impact with people who can be inspired and guided by our actions. These are marks to the changing nature of leadership today.

CHAPTER 4 QUESTIONS

Leadership in Transition

1. Describe a time when you took personal initiative that created an impact that surprised you in the difference that it made. Why were you surprised?

2. Do you see yourself as being in transition? Which one of the three dimensions of leadership seems to be the one that is in the most transition?

3. Are you a leader?

4. Are you a person who is taking personal initiative to make a difference that matters? Do you desire to grow as a person of impact? Where do you want to begin?

5

PERSONAL CHANGE– FROM TRANSITION TO TRANSFORMATION

It was never my intention to become an expert on change. Yet at each transition point in my life, I discovered something about myself that made the experience of change beneficial. Even in situations of change that followed failure or loss, I found that change was like living in a large house. It comes to us when we cross a threshold to enter a new room. The house is our whole life. Each room represents a part of the life that we have lived. All the rooms are our rooms, even when they seem different from one another.

Immediately prior to beginning this book, the room of my life that I had entered was one of hard, final endings. It was a time when the worldwide recession brought an end to my consulting business. I was fired by the nonprofit organization that I led, which then shut down its operation. In the midst of this, my marriage of thirty years came to an end. I remember thinking the day I moved out of the house, *"Everything is ending."* As I drove away, from somewhere deep within me, I thought, *"Something must be beginning."*

I know many of you have experienced similar difficult changes in life. You look back with regret, sorrow, and feelings of guilt. You may feel that life dealt you an unwinnable hand. Anger and bitterness have become a constant presence because the life you desired has not happened. The old saying that misery loves company we find not to be true.

These moments of change show us that life is a series of transitions. Some changes are marks of advancement. Others are a recognition that the conditions that we thought would remain constant throughout our lives have not.

The transitions we experience represent a way to understand the passage of individual changes that we go through in our lives. We are born. We go to school, transitioning from one grade to the next. We enter the workplace. We learn new skills, take on new responsibilities, and possibly move from one company to another. We marry, have children, and then they grow up, marry, have our grandchildren. We retire, as a new cycle of life begins.

Along this line of change are transition points that are milestones that help us make sense of our lives. Some change is welcomed, like the birth of a child or being hired for our dream job. There are also the changes that are a random, unwelcomed, confusing disruption of our life.

Avoiding change does not enhance our lives. It limits it. If we resist change, we can easily fail to see the potential that we have for making a difference in the world. The Circle of Impact developed as a model for understanding change because of the transitions that people and their organizations were experiencing. If you are in a life or work transition now, it can help bring clarity and direction to your life. One of the purposes of this book is that we learn that change is a transition and that, with intention and initiative, it can become transformational.

Transitions in life are not a series of moments in time. They are not like a collection of pictures in a photo album that we nostalgically remember. Our lives are much more like a long documentary miniseries. Each episode is one story within our life-long story of change and transformation. If we are not different, or better, by the end of the story, then we've missed something.

Seeing our lives as a film instead of individual pictures enables us to see the continuity that exists even in the midst of change.

When I went through my season of loss, as I came to call it, there were moments of joy and ones of sorrow. Each one helped me see that my life was not defined by the externals of owning a business or being married. It was my values, expressed in my desire to be a person of impact, that guided my self-perception. Even when I was at my lowest point, there were good things taking place. Years later, I look back and can see that the hard, emotional moments were showing me what I really wanted in life. And what I didn't. These moments of transition had the effect of purging me of the illusion that I am entitled to a happy, carefree life.

Similar to seeing our lives as a long film, we also experience it as a long, unfolding story. Each chapter contains its own story. We are the main character. Our story reveals a picture of who we have become in the situations that we encounter. It is a picture-story of our transformation as people of impact throughout our life.

If we can't see that long, grand story of our life, the Circle of Impact can guide us to create it. Each situation we encounter becomes its own Circle of Impact story. We encounter stories of need, problems, opportunities, and conflict where our personal initiative is the dramatic arch of the story and impacts the climax. With the foundation of our values, our life's story takes on meaning that transcends the moment of action. From these stories our legacy is formed.

The people in our story present relationships where our character is revealed. People see it when we take personal initiative to make a difference that matters: when we interact with them, work with them, have conflicts with them, solve problems together, or begin great ventures together. Our relationships are a central part of the story of our lives. Our family and friends see who we are. Sometimes they celebrate and other times they cry because we are not acting as our true selves. Some of them are our collaborators or coaches. Others may be our arch nemesis at work or an investor who helps us to grow our business. How we approach these relationships is critical to the outcome of our stories. Each chapter is a story of discovery, of challenge, hardship, and success. Each is a new story of opportunity to be our true selves.

By seeking to align our lives with the three dimensions of leadership, we are opening ourselves to solutions or resources that we need to grow towards our potential. The Circle of Impact model of leadership provides us this kind of universal guide to help us create today's story.

When we see change as transition then we can see our lives as a whole, not as a collection of individual moments in time.

Each story brings a lesson learned, a lesson to be remembered for another time, another story. The life we live can make sense to us. Change is not the enemy. It is simply a context in which our lives are lived.

Once we see that we are in transition, we can identify how the changes we go through can transform us from the person that we were to the one we desire to be. This has been my experience.

Seeing People in Transition

We learn to go through life's transitions by following other's example. The stories, throughout the book, represent ways of seeing change as a transition. In each case, the individual or their group has to make a decision to change. They do not accept change as just something that happens in their lives. Instead they come to see that change requires a shift in understanding about who they are and what they want their lives to mean.

Here are three stories of very different situations of change. In each, aspects of the Circle of Impact provide a way to understand how to cross the threshold of change.

Fred's Story

Fred found himself out of a successful national sales position when the company that he had served for forty years suddenly shut down. He began to look for a comparable job in the same industry where he could finish his career. Over coffee one day, he shared his situation with me.

Like other professionals facing a mid-career employment transition, Fred never thought he'd be out of a job only three years from retirement. When we talked, he was a year into spending his retirement savings looking for a new job at a comparable level.

When a job transition is thrust upon us, the Circle of Impact can help us. The first step is not to look for another job. Instead, we should ask ourselves, *"What is the impact that I've had throughout my career?"* This transition perspective can show us how our impact grew over time. With this story in mind, we can go and speak to potential employers saying, *"This is what I have to offer your company."* In the time that it took to drink a cup of coffee, we reframed Fred's pitch to potential employers just this way.

Is this your situation? Create a story of your talent, experience, and connections as assets which define your value to an employer. Fred was able to tell a story of proven ability and impact, not his need for employment. Within a few weeks, Fred found a new job in the same industry that carried him through to retirement. This transition point in his career is now complete.

Simon's Story

Simon was production manager for a global manufacturing company. He arrived home with news that his company wanted him and the family to move to another country to build and operate a new manufacturing plant. It was a major advancement for Simon. It was an even greater transition for the family. Three years later, with the plant up and running, Simon was called upon again by his company to take on another significant project. He and his family packed their belongings to return to the United States to a new job.

Values are the foundation of a culture of trust that families and organizations need. Simon and his family were able to adapt to change because their values clearly defined how they would face the transition each of them would experience. The transitions that they experienced became a source of adventure and discovery that made their family life strong and resilient as Simon's job took him into new work challenges.

The Circle of Impact is grounded upon a belief that values are the bedrock for our lives and work. Being clear about what we believe, we develop a perception of who we are and our purpose.

Matt's Story

Matt was a waiter at a local restaurant where I am a regular customer. I know all the staff well. Our conversations frequently touch on the transitions that we experience. It was not surprising that one day, while I ate a midafternoon lunch, Matt and I began to talk about change.

I live in a town filled with young people who love to ski, bike, mountain climb, and fly-fish. Matt was a bit older than most of those who worked with him. I asked him what the goals for his life were. He told me about his desire to get a medical degree and research doctorate so that he could to go into medical research. He had one major problem standing in his way. He had been turned down by every school because of an arrest for driving under the influence of alcohol on his record.

Matt, like many of us, made choices that inhibit the changes we want to make later in our lives. Matt's one mistake became an obstacle to his desire to have a life of impact within the medical world. Instead of change being the obstacle, the inability to change had become one.

A core principle of the Circle of Impact is that all our situations take place within the intersection of the three dimensions of ideas, relationships, and organizational structures. When the three dimensions are out of alignment, one or more of the dimensions make it difficult to fulfill our purpose. Matt's problem, as we discovered, was a structural one. Each of the schools' application processes used police conviction records as a way to reject applicants. Because of this system of qualification, he was turned down. He wasn't rejected because he was not qualified, but because he had a mark on his record that blocked his admittance.

As Matt and I talked, I drew the Circle of Impact on a napkin. I said, *"The solution to a problem is always in the other two dimensions. We first need to decide what kind of problem you have."*

Matt's solution to the problem of the medical school application was to change the story that the school was telling itself about him. To change this story, he needed to form a relationship with the people who decide medical school acceptance. Matt had to go to the school and say, *"Do not define me by my one mistake. Look at the rest of my record and my desire to become a student at your school."*

Two months later, I walked into the restaurant and there was Matt. Rushing over with tears in his eyes, Matt gave me a big bear hug. I knew then that he had been accepted into the medical school program. Matt's story became the talk of the town. For weeks, people would come up to me asking if I was the one who helped him get into school. With deep gratitude, I said yes.

Matt's story is not just about a transition that he experienced. It is one of the transformation of his perception of who he was, so that he could communicate that to the medical school. Whatever tragic or unfortunate situation seems to have a hold on your life, it is not the end of the story. The Circle of Impact is a tool that can help you overcome whatever obstacle stands in your way of becoming a person who can make a difference that matters.

Life's Transition Points

The stories of these three people in transition are special, but not unique. When we see the change that we experience as a part of a series of transitions, then we can begin to see that there is a larger story to our lives. A place to begin is in the recognition that some changes are normal and almost invisible to us. Other changes grab our attention. Yet we may not see them as a transition in life. Becoming aware of the situations that we are in is important for successfully discovering the other side of the threshold in the room that awaits us.

I find that people first experience change as an emotional experience. They feel unsettled about something. One afternoon I wrote down twelve transition points that I repeatedly heard from my clients. (See the **12 Transition Points** sidebar on the following page for the list.) These are some of the more notable transitions that we can experience.

These twelve transition points represent moments of change that are happening in our lives. When I began to share them with people, my assumption was that they would pick one. That isn't what happened. Many people picked two or three, even five of these transition points that they were experiencing. Many felt that they were losing touch with themselves.

12 Transition Points

1. What used to be easy is now hard.

2. We find that our performance has reached a plateau, neither getting better nor worse.

3. We are clearly not doing well, as our life and work are in decline.

4. We lose our job and must begin to look for what we are going to do next.

5. We are unhappy in our current life and work situation.

6. We are tired of doing the same thing over and over.

7. We don't know how to spend our time at work.

8. Our relationships are not healthy.

9. We are confronted with life decisions that have no easy answer.

10. We are thrust into a leadership role in which we feel unprepared.

11. We are entering a new stage of life.

12. We have a general uncertainty about life and work purpose.

They were unsure about the decisions that needed to be made. This intense kind of change was very disorienting. Seeing this take place, I realized that change is a far more complex experience than I originally thought.

Some of these transition points may creep up on us. We may think that this is just the way things are. We adjust and go about our business, accepting it as the new normal. Yet if we step back and look at the situation from a wider perspective, there is a genuine transformation of our circumstances taking place.

When this occurs, the Circle of Impact provides a helpful reference point for understanding the kind of change that is taking place. Returning to William's story in Chapter One, his transition point is number nine, *"We are confronted with life decisions that have no easy answer."* When viewed from the perspective of the Circle of Impact, the values that drive the decisions for William and his wife are about their responsibility to their extended family of children, parents, and grandparents. William's career is transitioning to be a secondary priority. The result is that, for William, the relationship dimension is the focal point of change, with two different changes taking place as he decides to leave the company and not move his family overseas. The first is that his self-perception changes from being a long-term employee of the corporation where he has worked for two decades to being an independent person seeking employment. Second, the structure of his work will change from one company to a new one. Both these decisions support his choice to place his family's interests ahead of his career ones.

Others who have gone through a similar transition find their priorities shifting from their career to their spouse's career. The resilience that is required for these very personal changes is built by having a clear set of values that inform what we look at in our lives and the transitions we experience.

How well we go through these transition points has everything to do with our self-perception. For this reason, we need to have clarity about what we believe and our purpose for impact. When Fred's company closed, and he was without a job, three years from retirement, the unwelcomed change affected his confidence about the future. Finding another job, an organizational structure problem, was not working. Instead, he needed a change in his self-perception. He wasn't just a salesman nearing retirement. He was a man who had valuable assets to offer a new company. From this transformational understanding of who he was, he found a position that carried him into retirement.

When we let change into our lives, we can embrace these transition points as a positive signal that new opportunities are just on the other side of the threshold of change. This is what I learned from my *"season of loss."* I found that everything was not ending. Rather, I found that I had been freed to see my life from a whole new perspective. My self-perception changed. I crossed a threshold that was transformational. For me, it meant moving across the United States and starting over with new relationships and a new focus on work that was better aligned with my desire for impact.

When we look through the threshold of the door of change, we see a future that is all potential. Nothing is fixed or final. All we must do is step into the change and allow the transformation to begin.

Seeing Our Potential

There is a widely shared perspective about change that states, *"People don't change until the pain of staying the same is greater than the pain of change."* This may be true in some situations. However, it is not what I see as the deeper reason for resistance to change.

People have such a difficult time with change because they see themselves in a fixed state. They don't change because they don't think they can change. Even as the world around them changes, they will always be this way. They are not necessarily happy about this situation. They just don't see a way to change.

They don't know how to change in a way that makes sense. Maybe it is here that the pain of change enters.

Are our lives at the mercy of change? Or are we agents of change? This is the most important question about our self-perception. When I define leadership as beginning with personal initiative to create impact, I am saying that you, me, and everyone we know can be agents of change. Even when we are afflicted with the kind of change described in the twelve transition points, we have choices to make that can affect change.

I am convinced that we have an endless capacity to change. If we choose to change. The question that I end up hearing in these conversations is *why* change.

The reason is simple. Within each of us are desires that drive how we approach our lives. We each want life to be personally meaningful. We want our relationships to be happy and healthy. And we want our lives to make a difference that matters.

Each of us is a person of unrealized potential. We are not containers of potential that get used up over time. We are people of endless potential. There is no way to know the full extent of our potential impact. The best we can do is try to fulfill as much of it as we can.

It is this belief about the endless potential of each person to create impact that turns our resistance to change on its head. To create impact is to create change. For this to work for us, we need to be clear about who we are, what matters to us, and the kind of impact that we want to create.

If we begin to look at our lives as always in transition, then we may just be able to see that our lives have an increasing potential for impact. Our lives are not just to be lived as a succession of meaningless moments, like activities written on a calendar. Instead, we need purpose for our life. The image captured in this idea of purpose is an unfolding of our potential as persons.

Take a road map showing the area where you live. Unfold it once. A small portion of the map may be visible. If that is all we see, then we may think that is all there is of the geography of where we live. Unfold it again and again and our awareness of the map's reach grows. It becomes bigger and larger with each unfolding. This is how our lives change to explore the extent of our potential. Each unfolding moment of impact reveals greater potential for our lives.

Ask yourself this question, *"Up to this point in my life, what percentage of my potential as a person has been fulfilled?"* I know few people who can answer this question. Yet it presents to us the idea that there is some upward limit.

Look again at the 12 Transition Points (see the sidebar on page 72). Each of those moments of transition represent a point in time. Within that moment, something is happening that is moving that person from where they were to where they will be. This is what I discovered about myself as I went through the transition that has led me to this point in my life. More than anything, I learned that I was letting my experience determine what my future was to be. Now I recognize, as I hope you will too, that our potential is open-ended, only limited by our imagination and belief in our capacity to create impact that makes a difference that matters.

There is no way we can know our full potential from where we stand at any one moment. We can only see it in retrospect. Looking back, we can ask, *"How did my performance at work* get better over the past couple of years?" There is an intuitive sense about this. We can't look backwards and see our impact fully. Neither can we look forward and see our potential fully. Our perspective is always incomplete. For this reason, being clear about our values and purpose for impact enables us to stay grounded in recognizing the impact that we are having.

Personal Transformation

When we choose to see change as a transition in our lives, we are also accepting the reality that change is personal. It isn't just something that randomly happens to us. It has a personal side to it that calls upon us to act according to who we see ourselves being. In fact, if we look at people of real accomplishment and significance, we'll discover that their lives of impact were built upon intentional individual changes. Their moments of transition reinforced perceptions they had about themselves and the life they wanted to lead. Life was never stagnant for them. It was always dynamic, moving, unfolding, and growing in dimensions of significance. Not all at once, but a step at a time, over time.

If this is not your story, if you are unsure about how to make the right changes in your life, look again at the list of 12 Transition Points. Several may describe the situation that you are in. It feels overwhelming to think that you can take some step of initiative and cross the threshold to a new life.

Maybe you feel that you don't know how to change. It feels so complicated and final, like there is no turning back. This is true for many people. You feel stuck in some relationship or job that you know is the not the best for you. Yet, you don't know where to find the confidence to walk through that door of change to become someone new. You wonder, *"Maybe I won't like the person I'll become."* Maybe you will. You can't know without stepping forward.

Indecision in the midst of transition can lead to decisions that compromise our values, which can erode our confidence even more. We feel embarrassed or humiliated. Or maybe we feel lost or alone in the decisions that we feel we need to make. Change is personal. It is a transition that is always available to us. You can decide to do one small thing that will change your life. Try something that will begin to take away any doubt or fear that you may have. You have taken one step already by choosing to read my book. Now, take the next step and decide to do something that is in keeping with your values. Start small with small steps of initiative. You have plenty of time later to grow big and change the world.

Personal Change—From Transition to Transformation

1. Look back over the past year. If you could have changed anything to begin a path of transformation, what would it be?

2. What is the one desire that you have that you want to see fulfilled? If you did reach that point of fulfillment, how would your life be different?

3. Look back at the 12 Transition Points. Which one best describes the transition that you are in? Do you see the door that you stand before? What does that next room in your life look like? Are you ready to cross the threshold? In the space below, write today's date, and the change that you see that you must make. Now set a date for when you will have crossed over into this next room in your life.

6

ORGANIZATIONS IN TRANSITION

Organizational leadership has for centuries been understood as a relationship between leaders and followers. The leader, at the top of the organizational hierarchy, leads the organization's followers through planning, delegation, and influence. It is this structure of leadership that has guided the modern organization through the past century of global conflict and change.

When we experience dramatic change, whether personally or as an organization, hidden weaknesses show themselves. We feel it on a personal level. Fear and insecurity grow. We sense that our organization is broken, and our livelihood is in jeopardy.

Change of this kind is now being felt on a global scale. Turn on the television and we see the flaws and failures of leaders whom we once trusted. Problems are politicized. Lines are drawn. People take sides in a fight for the future. Through all this, leaders seem small and inadequate for the world that is emerging. Along with the diminishment of leaders comes a sense that the organizations and institutions that we depend upon to provide strength and security for society may not be capable of leading this transition to the future.

We are at a transition point in human history. The way organizations have been structured is going through a transformation. The advancement of digital technology has enabled two parallel developments. One is the automation of skilled labor. The other is the computing power available to us. You and I have, in the palm of our hands, computing capacity that did not exist a generation ago. This change in human history is taking place on both a global scale and an individual one. The result is that our assumption that organizational leadership is about the leaders and followers is also in transition.

Two Global Forces

Two global forces are at work in this change, pushing and pulling against each other. The first is the pull to centralize global institutions, particularly those in finance and governance, into one integrated system of operation. This is the apex of the 20th-century hierarchical organization, where centralized control for planning and management efficiency is a prime organizing principle.

The other force pushes back through networks of relationships that distribute decision-making and management in a decentralized way. The scale and spread of global collaboration through networks of individuals is solving problems in the developing world, which a generation ago was not possible. This collaboration evolution creates an environment where we both lead and follow. Instead of a pyramid of hierarchical authority, imagine a web connecting people together from every direction for sharing solutions and new ideas and creating change.

Organizations in Transition

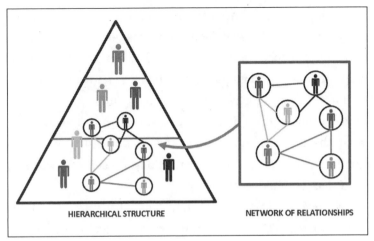

Figure 2: Two Organizational Structures

In some situations, these two forces are at odds with each other. Hierarchy and individual freedom often don't mix well. However, both forces need the other.

This figure illustrates the differences between the traditional hierarchical organization and the emerging world of global networks of relationships. They are not polar opposites. They are complementary structures that touch different aspects of how organizations function. Hierarchy represents the traditional structure of an organization. The network represents a social structure for business. We speak of this as the culture of a company or the human dimension at work. It is the relational context of an organization.

Leadership within a hierarchical structure is established by the role a person has within the organization, as seen in above figure. The activities of the organization are focused on its institutional integrity. Within a network-of-relationships structure, leadership is based on social trust, and the relevance of an individual's specific knowledge and experience to the current situation. The focus of the network is the impact of the relationships upon the purpose that has brought the network together.

From the perspective of the Circle of Impact, in a hierarchical business, the dimensions of ideas and relationships each serve the structural dimension. Organizational structure is the dominant dimension. Ideas and relationships serve a secondary or even a peripheral role.

Within a network-of-relationships structure, the three dimensions are aligned for the purpose of impact that defines the network. Impact is change. What is the change that a network-aligned organization seeks? What is the impact of ideas, or relationships and its structure?

It is the question about the impact of the structure that separates the network from a hierarchical organization. Take any vertically integrated business and ask what the desired impact of its structure is. Is it to produce efficiency? Or to maximize profit for shareholders? Take any organizational structure, of any kind of organization, and ask this question, *"What is the impact that the design of its structure is to produce?"* In my experience, very few people can answer this question. My conclusion to what I have seen for four decades of life in organizations is that this lack of an answer marks the transition to the next era in organizational purpose and its design.

The importance of this organizational transition is found in the transition that was described in the previous two chapters. The role of leadership is shifting from it being a function of organizational structure to one of human character and performance. This means that the future of organizations is in their transition to being leader-rich structures. By this I mean, even a hierarchical structure can create a leadership culture where each member is free and equipped to take personal initiative to create impact that makes a difference that matters.

The Experience of Change in Organizations

With this perspective in mind, the alignment illustrated by the Circle of Impact is possible in any type of organization. How then does an organization experience change in such a way that it can align its ideology, its people, and the structure of the business for impact? It first must accept that it is in transition. From that point, the future is open to making the kind of changes which can align the company for impact.

Here are three real-life situations where the structure of the organization was out of alignment, and difficult to see. Each story represents a problem seen through the lens of one of the three dimensions of the Circle of Impact. To bring the organization into alignment requires two steps of awareness. The first is determining which one of the three dimensions represents the critical need for change. The second is identifying how the other two dimensions provide resources and solutions to that critical need. The solution principle of the Circle of Impact is that the solution to a problem is not found in the problem itself, but in the other two dimensions.

An Unclear Perception: Sara's Story

Sara is a program manager in a local community nonprofit. She is well-liked, a hard worker, and has brought fresh energy to the organization's mission. Six months into her time with the organization, the executive director suddenly leaves. The board of directors asks Sara to become the interim executive director, while they begin their search.

This is the first time that Sara has headed an organization. She feels unprepared. She wants to give her best effort not to disappoint the board. The question is whether she is really ready for this new role.

Sara throws herself into being the interim executive with energy and enthusiasm. Her leadership style is all about motivation. She shares new ideas with the other staff, talks about her vision for their mission. To appear decisive, she makes some quick, unilateral decisions that surprise and disrupt the staff. She jumps into the role of supervisor with abandon, reframing staff roles without reference to the current operating plan. Staff and volunteers begin to openly criticize Sara. The situation grows more contentious as Sara's feelings of insecurity grow. The board steps in to provide clear guidance to Sara about the parameters of her job as interim executive.

What happened here? How did a situation with a promising young executive go so wrong? Sara clearly does not have, at this point, the necessary knowledge or experience to be an effective nonprofit executive. Her performance as effective program leader shows promise. But without clear instructions and mentorship, she will continue to founder in her role.

The other problem was that the board was ill-equipped to lead through an interim period. The previous executive, who had served in the agency longer than any of the board members, had never invested in the development of the leadership capacity of the board. In this respect, the board and Sara were both poorly prepared for an organizational transition that would need experienced leadership to manage it.

The Circle of Impact shows us that the board miscalculated in placing Sara in a position where she could not succeed. If they made this mistake in selecting an interim, there are real questions as to whether they are up to the task of selecting a new executive leader. The real source of the crisis is the board's lack of development. The critical problem—an ineffective board of directors paired with a young, inexperienced executive—is a structural problem.

The solution to this situation begins with the relational dimension of the Circle of Impact. There are two critical relationships that the board needs to address. One is with the staff. They are the strength of the organization. They are the ones who have contact with the public. If they are unhappy, the public will come to see it. It is important that the board reassures the staff that they are going to act in the best interest of the agency and its programs they direct.

The other relationship that the board must address is with Sara. She was chosen because the members felt that she was the best suited of the whole staff to handle the executive role. The board failed in not defining her job more clearly and not providing a mentor to assist her. The staff needs to see that the board stands with Sara and will work with all of them to prepare for the next executive director.

The second step is that the board needs to become clear about what its role is. This begins with establishing clarity about the agency's mission, its operating values, and its purpose for impact. The board needs mentorship, just as Sara does, so that as it looks for a new executive director, it is clear about what the job is and what kind of person they are seeking.

This problem did not originate with Sara or the current board. It began with the previous executive director. The board was selected during his tenure to support his position as executive director. It never learned to be a deliberative body. Whatever positive legacy the former executive director left with is now diminished because of a board that was not equipped to go through a leadership transition.

A Divided Community: Leonard's Story

Leonard is the new CEO of a consumer products company whose growth stalled during the last recession. The board hired Len because of his turnaround of a similar company. The key to Len's success was his ability to build relationships that crossed department boundaries, management levels, and pay grades. Len never assumes that he has all the answers. His first week in his new position, a steady stream of directors, managers, super-visors, and community leaders visit with him to let him know how things are done there. He listens. He asks questions. He takes notes. He begins to see a pattern.

Lisa is the company's director of planning and training. Like the others she comes in for her fifteen-minute first meeting with her new boss. Len asks her what her greatest challenge is as director of planning. She says, *"Getting everyone on the same page."* He asks for more detail. She responds that the company is a place of long-tenured employment. People begin in a certain department and never leave. Because the community is a great place to raise a family, people are willing to sacrifice advancement to remain with the company in a job that they know and feel secure in.

Len asks, *"Is there a problem with that? It sounds like we have very loyal employees who put the company high on their list of priorities."*

Lisa responds, *"Ordinarily that would be true. But what has developed over the past two decades is a kind of proprietary culture within those departments. They do their planning their way. Each year I have to translate their plans into the planning model that your predecessor liked to use. Frankly, in my opinion, the fact that we have not been growing cannot be blamed on the recession. Our chief competitors have done much better than we have in this regard."*

The first question for Len that the Circle of Impact can help him clarify is, *"What kind of problem is he facing? Is it an idea problem, a relationship problem, or a structural one?"* It could well be that this problem touches all three dimensions. Where does Len start to address this complex situation?

Utilizing the Circle of Impact, Len chooses not to address the idea of a compartmentalized management structure. Instead he decides that he will address the problem as a relationship one. Len does this by first meeting with his senior leadership team to let them know that he is going to spend the first six months of his tenure getting to know the company in preparation for a new product line initiative. As he spends time listening to employees, the rumor mill begins to notice that this new CEO is spending a lot of time asking people's opinion about things. Initially, this does not breed confidence, but confusion. Len has disrupted a long existing relationship pattern of top-down delegation, bottom-up accountability.

Three months into his new role, Len announces that the company is going to develop a new product line. A cross-discipline, interdepartmental team led by Lisa is formed to develop the plan. Each team member is loaned to the team from their department in the company. They work as a team one day a week, reporting to Len and his senior leadership team regularly, as a year later the new product line will be introduced to the marketplace.

Aside from the importance of a new product line to invigorate the company's market presence, Len's purpose is to prototype how the company will function during his tenure. He understands that he has to show the value of creating networks of relationships that cross the structural boundaries of the company. The success of the launch of the new product line, and the speed at which it was brought to market, demonstrated to some, not all, that a better way of operating was possible.

To consolidate the lessons learned in the new product launch, Lisa is elevated to Vice President for Planning, with the mission from Len and the board to create a new structural design of the company. The focus is on creating a structure for quicker product innovation and improved customer engagement. After three years, Len leads the company into the acquisition of their main competitor. He begins again the process of transforming a broken system of operation through relationship building and collaborative planning.

From the perspective of the Circle of Impact, resistance to change is a function of the structure of an organization. Simply changing the structure just makes people insecure and mad. Resistance to change in an organization is expressed by people defending the ways things are done. To affect change structurally, we focus instead on the relationship and ideas dimensions. The purpose is to create opportunities for people to see and feel something new that is more attractive than what they have now. In other words, when the pain of not changing becomes greater than the pain of changing, people will change. This is what Len understood and it is why he was a successful leader of change.

An Inadequate Structure: Rod's Story

Rod and two colleagues formed a business selling mechanical services and products to commercial and residential customers. They each had been employees of a larger company that supplied products to companies like the one they formed. They knew their business and were confident that they would be a success.

A conflict grows between them during their first months in operation. So Rod invites me to come work with them. As I describe the Circle of Impact, the three men see that they have a relationship conflict. As is frequently the situation, they see it as a communication problem. I would describe a relationship conflict as one where values are in conflict, communication is poor, and trust is missing. As this problem is developing, each of those reasons is becoming more evident. But you can't fix a relationship by focusing on better communication. The issues are separate. Poor communication is just a symptom of deeper problems.

When they established their business partnership, they agreed that they would be equal partners. They committed to make decisions based on consensus. The problem arose that, in the day-to-day operation of the business, they had no defined process for resolving differences of opinion. Their problem is a serious one that they cannot see. It is partly structural and partly perception of what it means to be an owner.

When a company's problem is a mixture of more than one of the dimensions, the solution becomes much more complicated. When each of the dimensions is in a state of crisis, as this company was moving toward, all you can do is decide which dimension's problem is the most critical. Address that and then move to the next most critical problem.

In their situation, the relationship dimension was the context for a pair of problems. Operating by consensus was not an efficient approach to managing the business. They had daily meetings to make decisions because they had not designated one of the partners to be the manager of the business. When I recommended that they select one to be the managing partner, they each rejected that recommendation because it would violate their commitment to be equal partners.

The values that they shared as owners did not align well with the structure of the business. It would be accurate to say that they did not distinguish sufficiently what it meant to be an owner of the business versus being an employee of it. This lack of clarity led the partner who was responsible for installation and service to complain that he was not being paid what the other two partners were being paid. They were both salespeople with additional responsibilities in the office. Their salaries were higher than the third partner. He felt that as an owner, he should be paid the same as them. They disagreed. The cost of replacing him would not be the salary that he expected them to pay him.

Eventually, the fulfillment partner left the day-to-day operation of the company and sued his two partners for the additional salary that he felt was due to him. The suit was eventually settled as the two remaining partners purchased his share of the company.

The lesson of this story is that alignment is not just an idea. It is a necessary condition for the health of an organization. In this instance, the relationship was broken because of a lack of clarity about roles and the structure of compensation. Today, my friend Rod has sold his share of the company to the remaining partner and returned to his former employer in a new role.

Seeing Our Brokenness

Many of the organizations with which I have worked over the past forty years were broken in places where they were not aware. Organizations fracture along the boundaries of the three dimensions of the Circle of Impact. Part of the reason is that we are not taught to see organizations as whole things, but rather as a collection of parts. Ideas are ideas. Relationships are relationships. Structures are structures, and structure is where we live in an organization. As a result, the structure perspective dominates and subordinates our relationships and the ideas that should guide our work.

These problems are both internally and externally caused. It is not that one business is broken and the rest healthy and whole. It is rather that the pace and severity of the changes that we are all experiencing are causing all sorts of conflicts within organizations. It is not just the push-pull of the global forces of centralization and networks. What our society needs from us as leaders of organizations is different than it was a generation ago.

In a time of change, organizations fracture along the fault lines of ideas, relationships, and structure. The more stress that change brings, the more evidence there will be of a broken organization. I learned the value of the Circle of Impact through my own problems and failures as an organizational leader. No one is perfect in this regard. We are all challenged to manage well. It is much harder when the pace and intensity of change is growing.

It may be helpful to see that our organizations are broken like a body is broken in an accident. We heal our organizations by aligning the three dimensions of the Circle of Impact. I intentionally use the word "heal" because I have seen so much hurt that happens to people and to communities when an organization becomes toxic. I am speaking of healing, rather than fixing a problem, because as a life-long fixer, I believe we have transitioned from a time when we can simply fix our organizations. They need healing and growth. We need to know what a healthy organization acts like, looks like, and feels like. I believe we are at the beginning of learning what it means to heal our organizations and by extension our communities and the world that surrounds us.

Bringing healing to our organizations begins with you and me, each of us, individually, being clear about the values that matter to us, and committing ourselves to finding people of similar values to help us build structures of impact that can provide a way for us to make a difference that matters. Do this and we create an alignment that begins the healing process.

CHAPTER 6 QUESTIONS

Organizations in Transition

1. Is your business or organization in transition? Describe what you see that concerns you the most.

2. What is the most pressing issue that you face today? What is the impact of that problem on your work or organization?

3. If you could change one thing about this problem, what would that be?

PART THREE

INSIDE THE CIRCLE
OF IMPACT

7

THREE DIMENSIONS
OF LEADERSHIP–
ALIGNMENT FOR IMPACT

A core principle of the Circle of Impact is the importance of organizational alignment. This alignment functions in the same way that it does in our automobiles. If our automobile's steering is out of alignment, we are pulled from one side to the other, always fighting to stay on track. Misalignment distracts us from the other conditions of the road that may well be more critical to our safety and success in reaching our destination. The same is true for an organization.

The structural dimension is typically understood to be the systems side of a business. In its most broad and basic explanation, organizational structure consists of a company's products and services, its operational systems, and its finance and governance components. It is what we think of when we talk about a business. From my experience, though, I have found the structural dimension to be two-sided. There is the traditional understanding of the organization as described here. There is also a social structure.

In many large organizations, there is a prescribed way that people relate. Call it a set of protocols that govern the interaction of people. Some are explicit in the processes of the organization. Others are unsaid expectations of the social culture that new people automatically are supposed to understand when they join the company. This structure is different than the relationship dimension, where much more of a network model exists. In the social counterpart to the organizational structure, the hierarchy of the organization dictates the social interaction of the company's members. This is one of those areas where the transitions that are taking place in the world are being felt by people in organizations.

The Reality No One Talks About

The lack of alignment between the ideas, relationship, and organizational dimensions fragments the way we can see the whole of an organization. Do we understand the impact that having a values statement and a clearly defined purpose for the company impacts the people who work for the company? Do we see the relationship between the company and its employees as simply a transactional agreement where people are hired to perform assigned tasks? Do we assume that a company's financial statement provides a complete picture of the health and future viability of the company?

This kind of fragmented thinking is quite normal. It is how we have learned to manage a complex world. It is also the source of many of the problems that we face in organizations. If we can't see the whole picture, then we can easily miss a critical need or opportunity. This kind of thinking is especially problematic when an organization enters a transition phase. The inability to see the big picture makes it more likely that someone or some department gets blamed for the problem, when it really is a product of a lack of alignment between the three dimensions of leadership.

Two decades ago *"systems thinking"* and *"systems dynamics"* were popular ways to view businesses as an integrated whole, not as a collection of parts. A *"systems understanding"* is a way to see how all the parts of an organization interact with one another. When we see how the dimensions of ideas, relationships, and structure impact each other, we are seeing a system in action. Families, sports teams, and cities are all organizational systems where investment in one area can have a positive impact in another. The Circle of Impact model is a simple, practical version of these highly complex systems.

To move from a fragmented perspective to one that can see the interaction of the parts of the organization requires us to have a focal point. Impact is such a point of integration. When we ask what the impact of our ideas should be, we are not just looking at them from the perspective of clarity and inspiration, as important as that is. We need to see how our values can build a culture of trust between employees and the company for a shared purpose for impact. For this to happen, our ideas need to help clarify what kind of structure is needed to focus each employees' efforts towards achieving the common goal of impact. In this sense, the structure of the business is a product of the ideas dimension. The purpose of the structure is to fulfill the company's purpose by providing each person a structure that enables them to fulfill their individual potential for impact. This is just one way to understanding how the alignment of the three dimensions is essential for the health of an organization.

Seeing Organizational Structure

"Why is our organization organized as we are?" This is a question about the essential purpose of a company. Most owners and senior executives can answer the following questions:

- Describe the products and services you offer.
- Describe the operational system that produces and sustains them.
- Describe the financial system that supports them.
- Describe the governance system that defines the company's purpose and goals.

A hidden question that is a more difficult one to answer is:

- Describe how these four aspects of the business are integrated into a system that serves the purpose of the organization.

It isn't an easy question. As with the context of where we work, we are so close to our organizational structures that we don't see them as they are. We see them as they immediately affect us. For this we need a framework that can incorporate all the parts without becoming so complex that we just throw up our hands and go back to thinking the way we always have.

To see the whole of an organization's structure, we need to see that all the dimensions of the Circle of Impact are always present and always influencing each other, as well as the whole.

There isn't just structure or just our ideology or just people operating separately. They are intermingled to such an extent that we need the focal point of impact to make sense of the whole organization.

Why impact? Simple. Because it focuses all parts of the organization on creating change that can be measured and evaluated from the perspective of alignment.

Seeing Social Structure

In a time of transition, when what has been certain within a business is no longer certain, the social structure is often where the conflict is felt, as well as where the leverage for positive change is found. This social structure is the human culture that exists in every organization. This structure is more than just the relationships that exist. It is better understood as the culture of the company and is formed by the impact of the active life of the Circle of Impact.

The social structure of a company represents how the people who work there have come to understand their relationships in relation to the purpose and goals of the company. A healthy culture enables the people of the organization to feel like a part of the organization, that their service to the company matters, and the company values their contributions.

The culture of a company is where the capacity for the organization to adapt to changing circumstances is developed. People adapt using the tools and systems of the organizational structure. They adapt their product offerings. They adapt operational systems to make them lean and efficient. They adapt their financial resources to those areas of highest leverage for success.

And as executives and board members, they adapt the purposes and plans of the organization to meet the opportunities of the future. This is how agility is built into an organization.

Creating Alignment: Dennis's Story

Out of Alignment

Dennis is the production manager for a small hosiery mill. For some time, he knew something was wrong. He knew that it should not take six weeks to fulfill an order for men's dress socks. His intuition ultimately led to a total restructuring of the manufacturing process for the first time in sixty years. Bringing the production system into alignment meant that an order could now be fulfilled in six days.

However, because the company was so out of alignment, Dennis could not see the deeper problems of the company. The family who owned and managed the company could not see the problems beyond the production process. No one could see it because their whole system was intentionally fragmented.

A question that every organization has to answer is, *"Why are we organized the way we are?"* It is a critical question because in modern organizations structure has come to define the purpose of the business. We think a lot about the parts of a business. We talk about efficiency, about innovation, about silos, about crossing boundaries, about leaderless organizations, and about organizational design. Each are concepts that may have some value in a particular situation. Yet they never dig deep enough to the more fundamental question, *"Why this structure?"* During my twenty years of organizational consulting, I never met anyone who was asking, *"Are we structured well for the business we are actually in?"* There was always an assumption that structure is structure. If we need to change, then we'll tweak it with incremental improvements. Until the company enters a significant transition, this perception rules.

When an organization gets stuck, like Dennis's textile mill was, the social structure plays an important role. In his situation, the social challenge was that all the executive-level members of the company were family members. The founder, now in his late 80s, still came to the office every day. His oldest son ran the company. His son-in-law was in charge of marketing and sales. Dennis, the son of the founder's sister, was in charge of production. Dennis's act to initiate change challenged the social structure of the family. The family was healthy enough and worked well enough, so that after considerable discussion, Dennis's change initiative was implemented.

The core function of the social structure is to provide a way for people and departments to function well together within the operating structure of the business. Where the social structure is weak or conflicted, a lack of trust grows, and misalignment happens.

For Dennis, the social structure was sufficiently healthy so that the company could begin to address the most critical weakness of the company. The fragmented state of the company meant that no one could really see the significant changes taking place in the marketplace.

The social structure in an organization is where leverage for impact is realized. A key to a healthy social culture is the extent that people at all levels of the company have the freedom to step forward and do what Dennis did. He took initiative to create change in a broken production system. How many companies fail to make changes because the people closest to the problems do not feel the freedom to speak up because they do not trust their superiors? When a healthy culture for leadership exists, opportunities for impact open up.

What, then, would a business structure look like if the expectation of all the employees of the company is to take personal initiative for leadership impact? If we want people to solve problems, collaborate beyond their immediate workplace, and innovate ways to make a difference that matters, then what kind of structure do we need? We need one where the social and organizational structures are in alignment.

Further Out of Alignment

Dennis's company was in such severe trouble because the family could not see beyond the father's original system of operation. Even as the world shifted from the age of industrialization to information management, they still saw themselves operating a hosiery mill. The misalignment of the production process was not the core problem. It was a symptom of a deeper fragmentation of understanding about their whole business. The broken production system was the perfect picture of this lack of alignment. In their system, the seventeen steps in the manufacture of a pair of socks were treated as seventeen separate internal enterprises. Each step had employees trained for that step alone. And every day, each step would produce inventory for the duration of that eight-hour shift. It is hard to see how a system could be more fragmented than this one. The legacy structure of production ruled the whole organization. The entire purpose of the company was to make socks, not sell socks. Making socks was the activity that defined the company. Walking through the mill, seeing inventory in place behind each work station, was a clear picture to all of us on the consulting team that the company was in deep trouble.

The core change to the production system was an understanding that they would only make socks for which they had orders. The company's primary problem was not the fragmented production line. That was merely the most visible symptom. The critical problem was that their core business was shrinking. They were structured as a textile manufacturer while other manufacturers were adopting information management technology strategies to manage their customer inventories in a just-in-time manner. This approach was never addressed by the family. They were still defined by the structure of a 1940s textile mill. They were socially structured around that mindset. To be anything other than that was impossible for them to imagine. They were prisoners of their structure.

The misalignment of the social and organizational structures of their business was the elephant in the room that no one knew how to face. In reality, they did not even know there was an elephant present. For Dennis's company, their inability to redefine their business structure meant that the company continued to decline until they had to shut down the machines and close the doors. A sad end to a once-vital employer for their small town.

Creating Change through Organizational Alignment

Alignment takes many forms. By alignment we are really talking about bringing together all the parts of an organization or a

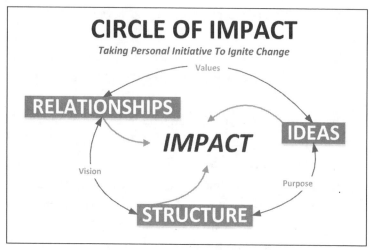

Figure 3. Circle of Impact

situation so that they work as a whole. Dennis's company never did accomplish this goal. They could not see their company in its entirety. Rather, it was a collection of parts, like the seventeen steps of the production line. Each part worked separately from the others. This, however, is not how a healthy, growing, sustainable organization functions.

When I designed the Circle of Impact, I intentionally separated the idea and relationship dimensions from the structural one. I did so because this is how problems in organizations came to me. This is how people viewed their organizations. They do not work well as a collection of self-contained parts and processes. Each segment of an organization influences other segments. The key to success is learning how to create the alignment that resolves the internal conflicts that make it hard to function.

The most important aspect of this alignment picture is to understand that people really do see relationships and ideas as separate from an organization's structure. I have heard complaints about how a manager leads her department. The problem is typically attributed to her personality. Ask a few questions and within a couple minutes it is clear that the way the department is structured makes it hard for everyone, even the manager.

By focusing on alignment as the Circle of Impact illuminates, a strategic shift can be made. We can move from the organization's structure being the default condition for everything in the company to letting a purpose for impact define every aspect of the organization.

We each need to ask the question, *"What is our purpose for impact? And, are we structured to achieve it?"*

This is the primary alignment question. We may be clear on what our values are, which ties us together as members of this organizational community. But if our purpose and the impact we want to achieve as a company are not clear and practical, then we end up falling back on structure for determining our purpose. To be aligned elevates the clarity of our purpose so that together we can achieve the impact that has brought us together as an organization.

Sometimes it takes an outsider to identify what an insider sees every day. Fish don't know they are in water until it becomes toxic. Think of the relationship of structure to the people within the organization: always present, yet never really seen, at least until it becomes toxic and people begin to suffer. We really only know there is a problem until it personally impacts us. If we never look at the big picture of what an aligned organization might look like, then we never get to the root of the problems that keep us from success. When we can't see the whole picture as problems arise, we look for a scapegoat (relationship dimension), because they are either higher or lower on the organizational chart (structure dimension), or because we have personalized the receptivity of our ideas or some program (ideas dimension).

To create alignment is to create change. It is change not just in solving one problem, but also in advancing each of the three dimensions of leadership in concert with one another. Here is how one organization did this.

Aligned for Impact: Frank's Story

Frank heads a professional membership association. Within the geographic region of his organization, there are approximately 800 potential members for his association. The association offers education and credential training, support services to the staff of their members' organizations, and participation in state and national associations. The problem Frank faces is a dramatic decline in membership over the past five years. The association membership fee is inexpensive. It has primarily been a vehicle to create a mailing list for communicating with members on industry issues and the sale of attractively priced insurance programs. The critical financial issue is that the participation rate of his programs is so low that they are reaching a point of unsustainability.

The association's board convenes for a daylong retreat to discuss their options. The board concludes that the traditional structure of a membership association is no longer viable for them. They need to become a member-engaged organization, placing a premium on the participation and contribution of members. This is a 180-degree flip in their perception of the purpose of the association.

As described, Frank and his staff were unaware of what the structure of their organization was actually like. It was designed like other traditional professional membership associations. They could not see that over an extended period their programs and services became less relevant to the life and work of their members. Their structure was the problem.

Without knowing it, but from a very intuitive sense of what needed to be done, Frank hired a consultant to survey their current, former, and potential members. In taking this step, Frank was sending a signal that his organization wanted to be in a relationship with its members. It didn't want just to provide products and services. What Frank and the consultant learned is that the stresses on professionals in their industry had grown considerably over the previous decade. The constituency for their membership wanted programs to help them balance their professional and private lives. From this perspective, the board instructed Frank to bring a plan back to the board that would incorporate this specific need into the mission and programs of the organization.

The result of aligning the three dimensions of leadership was not just that membership grew. In addition, this new approach put Frank and the organization into a position of influence in their industry. Two smaller associations within the region approached Frank about merging with his association. All this growth came because the leadership of the association was willing to listen to their constituency and change the structure of the organization to meet the expectations that they had.

Creating an Alignment Strategy

Aligning an organization is a change process. You first have to accept that your organization is in transition. Ask the questions, *"Are we in transition? Yes or no?"* The resistance to change is always present. People don't change naturally. They have to be led to see that change is necessary. The reality is that people don't change until the pain of not changing is greater than the pain of changing. For this reason, simply showing what the opportunities are in the future is not a sufficient reason to change. The prospect of change must relate to the company's core beliefs about itself, and how those are threatened by not adapting to the changing circumstances that they are in.

The second questions to ask is, *"What kind of transition are we in?"* By asking this question, we want to look at the three dimensions of leadership to determine which dimension is the one in most critical need of fixing. The reason we ask this question is that when an organization is out of alignment, one or more or all of the dimensions are out of alignment.

If it is not clear which dimension represents the greatest need for change, then ask this question: *"What is the impact of each dimension?"* By clarifying their individual impact, we begin to see what the impact of the whole organization should be.

By identifying the dimension in critical need, we look to the other two dimensions for the resources or solutions to assist the critical dimension to get back into alignment. Here's an example.

Realigning the Department: Jerry's Story

Jerry is the service manager for a large car dealership. He noticed that many of his best customers, some who'd been using the dealership's services for over two decades, were no longer bringing their vehicles in for service. He decided to conduct an informal survey of his best customers to find out what caused this change. Each told him that they had purchased their new cars from another dealer.

Repeat new car sales had historically come through the service department. The care and attention given to customers in the servicing their vehicle led to their continued loyalty to the dealership. Something had changed, and Jerry wanted to know what it was.

Jerry went to the general manager to address the matter. He outlined the situation and what he had learned from his informal survey. He wanted to know how to address the drop in service department business. The general manager told him that the new owners wanted to increase sales substantially. They were shifting their sales emphasis from in-store local customers to a regionally focused, volume sales process online. The implication for Jerry's department was that the new car warranty service would no longer be a major part of their business. He said, *"As a regional dealer, the importance of our service department for generating revenue is going to change. Any certified dealer can provide service to our customers."*

This transition in sales strategy meant that Jerry's service department could well lose some of his trained technicians and mechanics. The shift from the service department as a major profit center to a marginal cost center was troubling to Jerry. With the general manager's approval, Jerry developed a plan to realign the service department to be a stand-alone enterprise.

Jerry worked with his two assistant managers to create a plan for changing the focus of the service department. They made two sets of changes.

The first change was to develop a four-season maintenance program that they could sell to the public that reduced the cost of service to the customer over the lifetime of the vehicle. They priced the service to compete with local independent shops.

The second change required a shift in the positioning of the service department within the dealership. Jerry and his team recommended to the general manager and the owners that a rebranding of the service department as a stand-alone business could allow them to service vehicles from every manufacturer. The department would remain in the same location, still providing a direct connection to the on-site sales staff, and also be able to generate new business that did not originate through the sales process. He requested funds for rebranding, marketing, and new signage on their building. The change was approved, and the service department realignment was implemented.

The Impact of Alignment

The stories of Dennis, Frank, and Jerry show that the capacity for a company to change is directly related to how well the three dimensions of leadership are aligned. Having a clear purpose for impact that each dimension articulates is central to creating the alignment that leads to the company's desired impact.

I do recognize that this is a shift in how people think within an organization. They are used to seeing a fragmented system. They derive some comfort from it because it relieves them of having responsibility for the whole of the company's performance. The reality is that the simple days when we could afford for people to just do the work assigned to them have faded into the past.

Today we need a workforce of Circle of Impact Leaders. When each member of an organization is deeply engaged in contributing their best selves, the impact of the company grows. The result is an agile company that is not stuck with an antiquated system of operation. You gain a leader-rich company marked by a culture of trust and commitment. And you have a company that clearly understands that everyone can adapt to the changing circumstances of the marketplace.

Creating alignment is not a quick fix. It is a transition to the future of organizations focused on changing how leadership is understood and developed. In the next three chapters, we'll dig deeper into each of the three dimensions to see more clearly their contribution to creating impact.

Three Dimensions of Leadership— Alignment for Impact

1. Describe in one sentence a pressing problem, challenge, or opportunity.

2. What kind of problem is this? Circle one.

   a. Idea

   b. Relationship

   c. Structural

3. If you could resolve this problem right now, what impact or change do you want to see as the result?

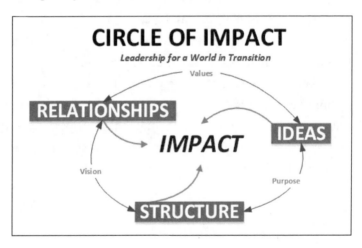

THE IDEAS DIMENSION–
CREATING CLARITY
FOR IMPACT

Over the years I saw a pattern repeat itself in all types of organizations. People expressed a feeling of not belonging or being out of sync with people at work. Doubts and fears about their job would grow. They would be told to expect a particular change, yet another would take place without notice. For other people, they would find an expectation for performance during an evaluation session that had never been assigned or discussed. As a result, no one was ever sure if the company was healthy or in good hands. I've heard this said so often that I know this is not a random, unique phenomenon. This is a problem that the Circle of Impact was designed to address.

This problem of being socially and organizationally disconnected at work comes from a similar perception that the rest of the world that is equally fragmented. This disconnection splits people, ideas, and organizational structures into parts of a hard-to-identify whole. Look at the organizational chart of a large business. The individual programs, products, departments, and structural levels can make sense to us. But what is the whole of the business? Is the business its product line? Is it its branding and marketing statements? Is it its people? Or is the company its customers, its leadership team, or its board of directors? What is it that makes up the whole of a company? What is that core element which gives the company its integrity? Is the company just a container for a collection of parts? Or is there something more there than the pieces?

Having spent years looking for a way to describe the whole of an organization, I came to the conclusion that in the modern organization, there is nothing at the structural level that constitutes the organization as a whole. It is a collection of inter-changeable parts that work best when aligned as described here. If our perception of an organization is that it is fragmented, then we are seeing the reality that we must face. Being able to see the company as a whole socially- and organizationally-inter-connected structure requires a set of ideas that help us to define what unifies all the parts into a whole picture of understanding.

The organizational wholeness that I speak of is essentially the social relationships that we have as human beings. We are connected to one another by our common humanity. We share similar desires, fears, interests, and notions about what is good. There is a unity that connects us together. Regardless of where we are from, our universal human experiences cause us all to laugh and cry for the same reasons. And the words that we use to communicate this shared experience form the ideas that provide a basis for the unity that aligns the whole of an organi-zation together.

Yet our organizations largely ignore this reality. Our businesses are fragmented into silos and protected turf to be controlled. In many places, leadership provokes greater brokenness because it isolates those who can influence the whole of the organization. Without attention given to the reality of our human connection, this brokenness produces an environment that is ideal for the aggressive pursuit of power that further fragments and corrupts the organization.

What is it that ties our connection to one another together? It is the same thing that helps us to know who we are: knowing our values, having a clear sense of purpose, and deploying a vision that unifies the whole for impact.

The Four Connecting Ideas

The ideas dimension of the Circle of Impact is based upon four connecting ideas. As ideas, they define how we learn how to live in the world. They are connected to how we think about ourselves and to the people and the work that we do. Their clarity and connection create a perception of who we are and our potential for impact that is difficult to do in any other manner.

As I write these words, I am not thinking of applying my fingers to each individual letter. I am thinking about the ideas I want to convey. My hands automatically type the right letters of the words that express those ideas. In all aspects of our lives, this is how ideas transition from a concept to a learned practice. If we see these four words as just ideas, then we may never see how they become embodied in us.

We know that trust is not just a word. We know it as something integral to our lives. We know it as much by its absence as we do its presence. When trust is a living part of our lives, we stop thinking about being trusting and trustworthy. We are trusting and trustworthy. It is an idea that has formed our character. If we have a relationship with a person where we always feel emotionally threatened, then intuition tells us to be wary. This feeling of uncertainty toward that person is formed by how the idea of trust has become a part of who we are. The presence of trust creates the social cohesion that societies need to be healthy.

The same is true in an organization. This is how we come to understand the human connection that exists in a business. If each of the four connecting ideas has a simple, practical application to the work that we do, then the social environment will transcend the transactional nature of business relationships.

Our values are not always conscious to us. We can be fragmented in ourselves, believing that a particular value is important to us, but our attitudes and behaviors reveal something very different. We embody values that we intentionally practice, and which our circumstances lead us to learn.

The practice of the four connecting ideas transcends them as simple ideas. They become embodied in how an organization functions. The difference is that these four ideas are not parts of a thinking machine. They are like the ingredients of a cake. Once the ingredients have been mixed together into a batter, they have lost their original form, to be transformed into something greater, more beautiful, and delicious. The whole is greater than the sum of its parts.

The four connecting ideas as living words become a whole reality. They are categories of ideas that guide us into a deeper understanding of the meaning of our lives. Once they become embedded in how we think, feel, respond, and act, our lives are transformed.

Look at the people you know. The ones who have a clear sense of purpose about their lives are different than those who do not have it. Their lives are fuller, more passionate, more focused, and less filled with fear, doubt, and low self-confidence. Each of these four ideas is essential to our welfare and that of our organizations and communities. They are the foundation for the practice of Circle of Impact Leadership.

Let's look more closely at each of the four connecting ideas.

Values

The values of a company are its bedrock beliefs. They are unchanging, nonnegotiable ideas that frame how the company understands itself. They are ideas that don't change during an executive leadership transition. Ideas like respect, dignity, pride, integrity, love, service, innovation, honesty, industriousness, agility, freedom, resilience, and trust transcend the day-to-day challenges that we face. These ideas are ways to carry us through times of change.

If a company claims that *"Integrity towards people"* is a core value. Then both the public and the company's employees expect a relationship with the company that is respectful, transparent, and trusting. Values that are practiced reveal the culture of the company. If the company's behavior is at odds with its stated values, then people see that the company *"values"* its values as a kind of hollow language lacking meaning.

There is not a choice between values and no values. Every decision, every action, every interaction that we have as individuals and as organizations is an expression of our values. We live in an age where nothing is hidden, there are no longer any secrets. As a result, we need to be more clear and vigilant in making sure that our behavior is a true reflection of what we believe. In an age where any comment can create a viral social media firestorm, the more integrated our values are to our actions as people and organizations, the more likely we can weather those storms when they occur.

This is why the values of a company are its ideological foundation. When a company has a communication problem, one of the reasons may well be the lack of integrity between their stated values and the practice of those values. Values don't exist in a vacuum. They live in the social context of a person or an organization. They live in our relationships with one another.

Values provide an understanding which informs the other three connecting ideas. Our purpose, our determination of what the impact of the company should be, and our vision for our work together are all based upon the values of the company. For this reason, values are the foundation for every aspect of the company's makeup. We can change the expression of our purpose, our understanding of our impact as circumstances change, and our vision can change and grow through the years. But the unchanging character of a company's values provides the ground for everything else in a company to develop.

Purpose

The word "*purpose*" identifies a focus that guides a person or an organization in a specific direction. A purpose statement needs to be carefully crafted as a representation of the seriousness that the company has about its intention in the marketplace. A company's purpose doesn't have to say everything about the organization. It has to say something essential that focuses people's attention on the meaning of the company and how people should relate to it.

A purpose in this sense is closely tied to the impact that a company wants to have. For this reason, an effectively conceived purpose doesn't describe what the company does. It is not an activity statement, like, *"We make things"* or *"We clean commercial offices."* These statements are internally-focused purposes. Maybe employees are confused about what the company does so there may be value in stating what the company does. However, that is not the reason for a purpose statement. That is the purpose of a values statement. The difference is that a purpose statement is directed toward the ambition for the impact of the company. A values statement describes why this ambition matters.

An effective purpose focuses the *why* of our values on their impact. *"Why are we making these things and offering these services?"* It is not sufficient to respond by saying, *"Because we always have."* Or, *"Because this is what our customers want."* The *why* question helps us understand the meaning of our impact.

For example, a purpose statement that reflects not only the impact we want to create, but also the values that guide us there, could be like this one:

"We handle the details so you are free to pursue your dreams."

This statement does not describe what the company does. It does describe the impact that it wants to create for its customers. This company could be a software company, a cleaning service, or an in-home professional chef. It could be a company that provides virtual assistants to business owners. It could be many kinds of companies. If freeing people to pursue their dreams is the company's genuine purpose for impact, then the range of services that the company could provide can be even broader. By defining its purpose in this way, it opens possibilities that could not be envisioned if the company's purpose is defined by what it does. This is why it is important to be clear about the impact that we want to have.

Impact

Impact is a change that we create that makes a difference that matters. No change? No impact! This is why a positive, proactive approach to change is essential. Focus solely on results or measurements and we miss why impact matters. Impact is not just a measure of activity, but it's a quality of change that we create.

When impact is the focus of our purpose, it changes the way we perceive our work. We become less inwardly focused and more focused on how we are changing the environment for the receptivity of our products and services. An organization may describe its impact this way: *"We fed 1,000 underprivileged children this year."* We should celebrate this impressive result. However, if the same organization said, *"Because of our feeding program for underprivileged kids, sixty percent of them are now testing better in school than they were before our program began,"* now our impact is having a revolutionary impact upon the children and families of our community. Impact is the change that matters beyond the numbers.

Impact is not the activity, but the effect of the activity. It isn't the feeding of the children, but the effect the feeding program has upon their physical capacity to be better learners in school. Describe your impact as a story and people see a whole picture of what is going on. They can see a child at home enjoying homework. They can see the warmth of appreciation from the parents whose children are doing better because they are healthier. Your employees take greater pride in being part of an organization doing amazing things. This is the power of impact to convey the values of a company.

I meet people all the time who love the idea of impact. I ask them in response, what is the impact of your business? They don't have an answer. The idea of impact has an emotional resonance which needs a grounding in values and the practical direction of a purpose.

Vision

Think of a vision not as a snapshot in time—*"We envision growing from three stores to six in two years."*—but as a video that shows the impact that you want to create.

Our vision for impact isn't just about what we want to achieve in three years. It is the image of all of us working together today to achieve that great goal. A vision from the perspective of the Circle of Impact is what people do through the organization's structure to create impact. It is *our* vision, not *the* vision, our vision of what is possible when we come together to create an impact that makes a difference to our customers, our community, and even to us.

A vision from this perspective provides everyone a connection to the whole of the business so that they can understand how their own individual contribution matters. If one person can envision this, then we all can see how we can take personal initiative to make a difference.

The four connecting ideas are the source of awareness of the depth of relation that is possible in an organization. The following story shows why having a simple, practical set of four connecting ideas provides a basis for healing a broken and fragmented organization that did not even know that it was.

Creating a Team Culture of Trust: Brian's Story

Brian was hired as the new executive director of a prominent sports-oriented nonprofit in the city where he had been a professional athlete. The board's rationale for hiring him was that his connections and reputation in the city would elevate the organization's fundraising presence. Brian was not a trained fundraiser, but he was a natural networker. He was hired to be the face of the organization as it expanded its programming reach throughout the city.

As often happens, the best intentions of a board for the future of its organization can conflict with the current reality of the organization. Almost immediately, Brian faced resistance to his leadership from staff members. They viewed the board's new vision with skepticism, believing that they knew better where the organization needed to grow. Resistance to Brian's presence came in two separate actions.

The first act of resistance came from withholding critical information about programs. The second, more significant action, came as two of the senior level staff went directly to board members whom they counted as friends and supporters to make the case for Brian's removal. They were turned back and told that they were out of line.

Both actions were clearly politically motivated. Brian was not a neophyte executive. He had owned his own sports marketing business while playing as a professional. When he retired from playing, he sold his business. The transparent nature of the staff's resistance to his leadership was immediately evident.

In dealing with these two acts of insubordination, Brian knew that how he responded would set the tone and direction for the organization going forward. In relation to the first action of withholding information, he met with the staff responsible for this resistance. He told them that they had a choice. Act with integrity or resign. He gave them a week to provide him the information that he had requested. They agreed to do as he asked.

The situation with the two senior staff, who sought his dismissal, was a more serious and delicate one. After discussion with the board, Brian terminated the two staff members. The following morning, he gathered the remaining staff to inform them of his actions. One person after another came to him afterwards to thank him. When he asked why, each responded in the same way: *"Those two have been trying to run our lives for a long time."*

A Team Concept

Brian was not blindsided by these actions. His long athletic career had taught him the importance of what it took to create a winning, high-performing team. He had seen in his interactions with the nonprofit's staff during the interview process that they were not a team, but a collection of individuals doing the jobs they were hired to do. Brian looked at the organization through a lens of teamwork. For him, the four connecting ideas were essential ingredients in creating a team that could reach beyond its own self-perceived limitations to accomplish significant results for their community.

In his meeting with his staff, Brian told them,

"I was hired to do a specific job. I was not hired to do your jobs. We need each of you to do what you were hired to do in the very best possible way. I freely admit that I don't know how you do what you do. I do know why you do it. You care about the people who benefit from our programs. As long as you are honest, give your best, and put our people first, then I'll be your greatest champion. And, I hope in time you'll become mine."

Brian was not initially concerned about the program structure of the organization, but rather, the relational one. He saw the disconnection within a staff. He knew that he could not call his staff to be a team unless he lived the values that he espoused. So, he spoke honestly and directly to them. In so doing, he was sending the message that he could be trusted.

Brian was appealing to a value system that he felt was missing in the organization. Values of self-respect and mutual contribution for the greater good, along with open, honest communication were ones that he felt were essential for a high-functioning team to meet the challenges and opportunities that they faced.

A Strategy of Embodied Values

The identification of a company's values is an important function of the Circle of Impact. For out of those defined values a vision for fulfilling a purpose for impact is derived. However, it isn't the words themselves that matter, but the life of those words in action.

Brian, in his interaction with his staff, emphasized several values that would guide their relationships. He spoke of honesty, giving one's best, and putting people first. In his disciplinary actions with the staff members who were insubordinate, he embodied those values. He demonstrated that honesty is intended to serve the greater good of the organization. The staff who personalized their displeasure with the leadership of the organization placed their own interests ahead of the organization. It is not whether their opinion is correct or not, but whether that opinion is expressed in a respectful, constructive manner. Brian showed that the entire staff can trust him to treat them fairly.

Brian entered an organizational setting that was fragmented. It was not evident to the board because the problem was not a structural one. The organization was clear about its purpose, its programs strong and well-received in the community. His first step in bringing alignment to the organization was to show the staff that they could trust him.

In all alignment situations, one of the dimensions is recognized as having the more critical need than the other two. In Brian's case, the relationship dimension was the crisis point. His approach was to elevate the value of trust and apply it throughout the employee structure of the organization. His act of tolerance for those who withheld information contrasted with his termination of the staff who sought his dismissal, showing that he had a set of values that would consistently be applied in the organization. From that, trust is gained.

The staff were a mix of people, some who sought to control their fellow staff members, and others who felt victimized by an unhealthy work environment. The former executive director had been a passionate advocate for the organization but was easily manipulated by the staff. While words matter, their living application in the attitudes and behaviors of people are what solidify people's connection to one another. This is what Brian had learned through his professional sports career, and it's what set him apart from his predecessor.

Aligning for Connection

The four connecting ideas, when aligned, create a wholeness within an organization. They merge into a single, whole reality. We stop thinking about what our values are, or what our purpose for impact is, or our vision for the future. There are documents that can be created that capture these ideas in a clear form for distribution and communication. But when they align into one reality, they become second nature to us.

One way to speak of this reality is as a type of situational awareness. When our values and our purpose for impact become embodied in us, we can walk into situations and know immediately how we are to respond. This is why Brian was able to respond to the insubordination of staff so effectively. His situational awareness was born of having embodied a set of values that define his life. As a result, there is a high level of integrity between the beliefs that Brian has and the way he conducts his life.

If we were to talk with Brian about his capacity of this kind of leadership, we might ask him, *"How did you know what to do when you were threatened by the very people you were hired to lead?"* He may respond in a manner like this.

> *"My integrity as a person is based upon the values that became important to me through my sports career. I learned to trust those values because they served me well in a highly competitive environment. They enabled me to become the leader of our team, and to create a successful marketing company. It all has to do with your values defining the person whom you want to be. The values cease to be words on paper, but a living connection to the way I want my life to be. I am convinced that this is what is possible with our organization. Together as a team we will live the values that will enable us to have the impact that we want to have. How will we know? We'll know because of the impact that we will see in our relationships through the programs of the organization."*

The human connection that exists between people is something that is alive, that touches us in a way that the basic transactional relationship of business cannot. We find that the freedom we need to take personal initiative for leadership impact is present. We find that our capacity to make a difference continues to expand. We learn that the past structure of our organization was a limiting factor upon our organization being able to reach its potential.

We start to discover this reality in an organization by discovering that our values are non-negotiable. They are the rock-bottom foundation for everything that is built within the organization. Our values are the core strengths of our personal lives and the lives of our businesses. We will know that we have discovered those bedrock values when, like Brian, we can say,

"We are willing to sacrifice this opportunity in order to maintain the integrity of the values that we have come to believe are our key strengths."

When we can say no to a bright, shiny opportunity that ultimately may compromise our company's future, then we know that our values are now alive in who we are and the impact that we create. The impact of the four connecting ideas alive in us and our organizations is that we now have a clear perception of what our focus is. With this clarity, we can align ourselves with the other two dimensions to achieve the impact that we desire.

CHAPTER 8 QUESTIONS

The Ideas Dimension—Creating Clarity for Impact

1. What is the one value that is the most important one for you?

2. Do you have a clear purpose for your life or for your business? If yes, write in the space below.

3. How has your perception of what is important to you changed over the past few years?

9

THE RELATIONSHIP DIMENSION–CREATING TRUSTING RELATIONSHIPS

When someone tells me that their organization has a communication problem, I know that there is an alignment problem. Good communication comes from having a clear message, tuned to the people who will receive it and respond, and delivered in a form and a manner which the recipients will understand and appreciate. Good communication in this form is an alignment of the four connecting ideas of the Circle of Impact and of the three dimensions. The impact of good communication is trust.

Communication problems cut across all three of the dimensions. If it is an issue in your organization, what kind of problem is it? *"Is it an ideas problem, a relationship problem, or a structural problem?"* Is your message clearly stated for impact? Do you not really know the people with whom you are trying to communicate? Is your form of communication well suited for them? Regardless of which of the three dimensions of leadership is the most critical, we must address the relational dimension. It is here that solutions will either be embraced or rejected. The higher level of trust that exists, the greater likelihood that the solution will create good communication.

The Relationship Dimension and the Four Connecting Ideas

It was my first meeting with the team organized to create a values statement for its company. The team was a mixture of executives and union officers. I began the process by asking them, *"How far back in time do we need to go to when you were a happy company?"* The union president quickly spoke up. *"Twenty years!"* I followed with, *"What was the company like then?"* He said, *"We were a family. We did things together. We played softball. We had company picnics. We knew each other and cared about one another."*

As I soon learned, two decades before, a new executive team had been hired with a mandate for change. The family culture was one of the casualties. Now, a new CEO was in place after the departure of the former team because of a financial scandal and the embarrassment it brought to the company. The new CEO and a reconstituted board also had a mandate for change. Their mission was to heal a broken culture to strengthen the company's position to grow either through its own program of acquisitions of other companies or by being acquired itself. They chose to start the healing process with a values statement.

As we worked through our discovery process, it was clear that re-creating the family culture was not our goal. The culture of the past, which was remembered so fondly, was a product of conditions unique to that time. Our task was to identify a set of values that could be tangibly applied throughout the management culture of the company as it now existed. In other words, our job was to create a foundation of trust that would heal the wounds of the past in practical, tangible ways.

Organizations initiate values processes all the time. Unfortunately, just having a values statement doesn't typically translate into a change of behavior or strategy. They are words—ideas—that are meant to have an inspirational quality to them. Print it on cardstock and post in the break room. Many of these values processes are like me washing my car and expecting it to get better gas mileage as a result. Values are not stand-alone ideas. They are part of a system of ideas that are practiced in the relationships of the organization. This practical ideology is the core strength of the integrity of the organization.

The Circle of Impact focuses on creating a relational culture of trust. Our values inform what our purpose for impact is and unites people with a shared vision for impact. All this interaction among the four ideas takes place within the social and organizational structures of the company. Alignment creates the conditions for trust.

When the Circle of Impact becomes a learned practice, a culture of impact results. The organization that Brian, from the previous chapter, found when he became its executive director was not a relational culture of impact. As he quickly discovered, the social structure was in crisis, the purpose of the organization focused on preserving the status of senior employees, and integrity and trust were missing. An outsider may not be able to see this reality, but inject a disruptive influence into the mix, like a new executive, and an unhealthy system responds in a manner that exposes its vulnerability.

Brian's first task was to develop trust in his leadership. The relationship dimension was out of alignment with the basic requirements of a high-functioning organization. Trust was missing from their relationships as well. Before he could build a culture of trust, Brian had to build trust in himself. This is particularly important for executive leaders to understand when their organizations are in transition.

When people act in a self-serving way, as some of Brian's staff did to undercut his leadership, it destroys trust. Trust is hard to build and easy to break.

In a team context, trust is a mark of the integrity of the team. In these few words Brian spoke to his staff, he signaled to them that he enters a relationship with them assuming that they are worthy of his trust. He says to them:

> *"I was hired to do a specific job. I was not hired to do your jobs. We need each of you to do what you were hired to do in the very best possible way. I freely admit that I don't know how you do what you do. I do know why you do it. You care about the people who benefit from our programs. As long as you are honest, give your best, and put our people first, then I'll be your greatest champion. And, I hope in time you'll become mine."*

Brian is laying out the parameters for how trust will govern their relationships with each other. They are to depend upon one another, not out of weakness, but out of the opportunity for greatness. This is how integrity operates within an organization.

The Hidden Secret of the Circle of Impact

Organizations that are dysfunctional, like Brian's, are not dysfunctional just in one way but in many ways. Values feed purpose, relationships, vision, and the social structure of an organization. If the values are vacant, compromised, or corrupted, then the impact of that weakness gets passed throughout the whole organization like a virus. Even the most ethical, committed, trustworthy manager will find herself placed in positions of compromise and conflict. Having talked with dozens of people who are in positions like this, I found that they hate it. They lay awake at night fretting over their own contribution to the problems that plague their organization. They long for a time of integrity, respect, and trust at work.

Here's the secret of the Circle of Impact. For it to be a model that helps a business to function at a high level of performance, realizing its potential never before imagined, it requires one thing: It requires leaders who embody the model's four connecting ideas.

In the process of creating a values statement for the company that had gone through the executive scandal, there was a moment at the end of the process when the fortunes of the company turned. In the whole history of the company, it was a small moment. But for the planning team, it was a transformational one that carried on to each following stage of change.

After three months of work on a values statement, with only an hour before our time for meeting was to conclude, we did not have a statement. Even though the previous day I had invited every member of the task force to write a statement and bring it to our last meeting the following day, only two did. I realized that the success of this process weighed in the balance. I acknowledged this to the team. There was still a sense of fear present from the mistrust that had haunted the company for two decades. Cultural change comes slowly in a corporate environment.

With an hour to go, I asked the two members to write their statements on a flip chart and hang the pages on the wall. As they did that, I offered to the rest of the group a last chance to contribute their own statements. Three members quickly wrote down what was to them important for the company to become. Each of the five authors gave a two-minute presentation on their statements. I gave each member of the team five votes, which they could allocate any way they wanted. After totaling the votes, one of the statements written the previous night was the clear choice. I asked the task force if this choice was a consensus one. It was. One of the members went down the hall to the CEO's office and requested that he join us.

He walked into the room and looked at the five statements, the vote totals were hidden from view. With the group's permission, I asked him his choice. He immediately chose the one that they had selected. Relief and celebration flooded the room. A couple members commented that it felt like the way the company was twenty years earlier.

It was a pivotal moment of coming together for this company that once was broken and now on a path to significance and healing. For this new CEO to affirm what they wanted was a very gratifying moment for the members of the team. It reinforced their impression that this man was one whom they could trust to follow into the future.

People who embody an alignment of the four connecting ideas can immediately enter into a broken, fragmented corporate environment and make a difference that matters. They bring a quiet confidence to their role that builds confidence throughout the company. This is the impact that this man had on the company. Within two years, after the implementation of a new leadership training program, the company was recognized as one of the most trustworthy companies in the nation.

The secret of Circle of Impact Leadership is that each of us can be that person. To be that person we have to recognize that half measures won't work. We have to be all-in if trust is to be the product of our leadership.

What Is a Relationship?

A relationship is a connection. Most of the time we speak of this as between people. But it is also true that we are speaking of it in terms of our connecting to places, to organizations, and even to ideas. To say we have a relationship to a place, like our home or some place of natural beauty, is to say we care about it, and the integrity of our relationship demands that we do things that preserve its health and vitality.

If trust is the core value of our relationships, then I must ask myself, what does it mean to act trustworthily with integrity towards all those people, places, organizations, and ideas to which I am connected?

A friend of mine described to me two kinds of relationships that he found as the head of a nonprofit organization in a large metropolitan area. The first kind of relationship is with those people who only want a transactional relationship with the organization. If you ask them, they may sponsor a kid to go to camp or make a contribution to a building campaign. But they expect something in return. There is a quid pro quo relationship there. The other kind he called a transformational relationship. These are people who ask, *"How can I help? What do you want me to do?"* They invest in their relationships. Contributions are valued, but investment creates impact.

Brian understands this perspective. In his conversation with his staff, he is telling them that his relationship to them and their organization is not simply a contractual one. Instead, he is telling them that he is investing his confidence and support in them to make the organization function at a higher level than it ever has. When he tells them that he is their champion, he is laying down a marker of trust. He is putting his reputation on the line for them. He is a transformational leader because he invests in the relationships.

A relationship, therefore, is a connection to someone where what you share together becomes a bond of friendship and mutual commitment. In business, we rarely talk about staff and supervisor relations in terms of friendship. We don't out of fear of personalizing a business relationship, which makes it more difficult to make a hard business decision if it concerns a friend.

These relationships take on a different character of friendship than they would if we were friends from college or lived down the street from one another. In an organizational context, its purpose is a central, organizing factor within the social context of the business. We are not just friends in some random sense. Our friendship is informed by our shared commitment to serve the place where we work.

What we share is an understanding of the meaning of the four connecting ideas of values, purpose, vision, and impact. Imagine going to work and knowing that all the people that you work with share a common ideology of impact. Imagine not just how dynamic that would be, but imagine how good communication would become, and how the typical conflicts that arise in business would be lessened.

The challenge of creating relationships of this kind is that most of us have been conditioned to treat our relationships on a transactional basis. By extension we treat our work as an extension of that relationship. From this perspective, we treat people as a means to an end, as utilities for meeting my goals, not yours. Your goals don't matter because mine matter more than yours. It is the wrong kind of competitive environment within an organization because it tends to become predatory. What keeps organizations from falling into outright chaos is that there are people within the organization who choose not to operate this way. In fact, based on my interactions with people at all levels of organizations, most do not want to operate this way. It overly complicates their work life. They long for the kind of integrity exhibited in Brian's leadership.

The Relational Difference That Matters

The character of our relationships is a product of the character of our individual lives. When my friend described the two kinds of relationships, transactional and transformational, he was making a distinction that is often hard to define. Every relationship, whether in business or private life, has a threshold that awaits our crossing. It is the threshold of openness, vulnera-bility, and mutuality that leads to our being persons of impact.

When Brian spoke of his staff as a team, he was not simply using a well-worn sports analogy. He was saying something about their relationships to one another. When the union presi-dent described the company twenty years earlier as a family, he was saying something about the kind of relationships that they had with one another.

Here the distinction between transactional and transforma-tion has meaning. In the former, all one requires from the other person is an exchange. In the latter, the relationship is one of engagement. It is personal. Not in the sense that we personalize situations to be about us. But rather, we cross a threshold where your life matters to me, and mine to you.

It is in this context where the alignment of the four connecting ideas begins to create the impact that matters. For when our lives matter to one another, the purpose of our work together, the values that unite us and guide us, and, most signifi-cantly, the impact we achieve together, take on greater meaning. When it does, we are acting as a team, a company, a family, even a nation with integrity.

If all our relationships are transactional, we see others in a more competitive sense. We are seeking to gain something from them with the least amount of buy-in.

Brian replaced an executive director who grew the program through a transactional management approach. The staff culture was one where each person understood that they had to make the case for the value of their work, not just to the executive director but to the staff. As a result, the organization attracted ambitious people. Their ultimate mission was their personal ambition, not the mission of the organization. The executive director was asked to resign because the organization had failed to respond appropriately to a miscommunication with a major donor. What should have been a simple problem to resolve with humility and grace became a conflict between the donor and the organization. The executive director was adamant that the donor was wrong. He stood his ground, claiming that it was for the integrity of the organization, when in truth it was harming that integrity. He did so because he viewed all his relationships through a transactional lens. In so doing, it cost him his job and the organization a valued donor.

During Brian's first months as executive director, he displays the hidden strengths and excellence that a good coach brings out in his players. He sees himself as the coach of the organization, with his staff and the volunteers of the organization as the team on the field. He speaks in terms of affection for his team, elevating their game to new levels.

It isn't just that he is a transformational leader, a person of integrity, whose personal values, purpose, and vision for impact are well aligned. What is it about his character that makes him a person of impact, not just based on his intentions, but his actions?

Creating a Company of Leaders

The purpose of alignment is that we bring together all facets of an organization to work as a whole. Who does this? The structure doesn't do this. Words in a values statement don't do this. People do. People in relationships with one another.

After the new values statement was approved by the CEO and the board of the company, a plan was implemented that took each of the identified values and developed a program of training for middle managers and supervisors. The intent was to translate the values into specific behaviors and actions that could become a part of the company's management plan. The uniqueness of this plan was that it began with the skilled workers of the company. The effect was the restoration of a culture of trust. It wasn't just a revamped training program that accomplished this. It was also the intentional actions of the CEO to build relationships with people at all levels of the company. The CEO's efforts to get to know the men and women of the company on a first name basis preceded the values process. By the time the statement was ready to be released, his open, congenial presence had signaled that a new era in the company's life had begun.

The story of Senior Vice President Barry, in chapter two, took place in the same company at the same time as the values statement process. It was one of the incidents that was the impetus for a training program to equip middle managers and supervisors with the skills of leadership development for those who reported to them. This company came to believe that grassroots leadership that makes a difference is not only possible, but essential to the health of a company. Where grassroots leadership development fails in companies, it is often for two reasons. The first is training that does not free the employee to practice leadership initiative. The second reason comes from the lack of alignment of the three dimensions of leadership of the Circle of Impact.

In the past at this company, resistance to taking personal responsibility had grown as an expression of the lack of trust.

The new training program focused on two outcomes: first, to reestablish trust throughout the company; second, to equip people at all levels of the company to take personal initiative to create an impact that matters. The development of leadership initiative throughout the company focused on three outcomes.

The critical need for change was for developing the capacity for problem solving throughout the company. The paralysis that marked the conflict between Marvin and Sam, that Ryan could not resolve, could be avoided in the future if each of them were given the training and the permission to take initiative to resolve the problems that they faced.

A second area of change was in improving communication company-wide. The training focused on equipping individuals and teams to initiate conversations for perspective and information. The benefit of expanding the reach of interpersonal communication was that the culture of trust that had begun with the values statement process, grew.

The third need was to develop the practice of innovation and process improvement. The contentious issue between Marvin and Sam is ultimately about which of them is responsible for the machine. The reality is that both are responsible, yet neither had the authority to resolve the issue. Empowering employees to improve their own work processes had the effect of increasing both efficiency and trust. The effect was to strengthen the company's position as it entered into negotiations to be acquired by a larger company.

Self-confidence in an organization has more to do with the relationship of the person to the company than it does their ability to do a job well. As I have seen in too many situations, internal political realities often breed a lack of confidence and mistrust because people realize that doing their job well is no guarantee of security. The key to enhancing self-confidence is in freeing people to do their job. Then provide them the training for the skills that they need to practice leadership initiative.

For executive leaders to dispel a culture of fear, they must do things which demonstrate that they have their employees' best interest in mind. This means that each person has been released from the fear of making a mistake that will humiliate them in the eyes of their coworkers. In too many work environments, people feel that no one has their back. This is true from the top of the hierarchy to the very bottom.

Accompanying Barry's story in chapter two is a stand-alone piece called **Five Steps to Get the Best from Your People**. These five actions represent the goals of a training program that seeks to instill Circle of Impact Leadership throughout the whole of an organization. The five steps are:

1. Believe in them so they will believe in themselves
2. Free them to do their best work
3. Trust them
4. Thank them personally
5. Honor them

The shift in mindset that took place in both Brian's and Barry's organizations was from a transactional culture to a shared culture of trust. The impact of a relational culture of trust is that it produces Circle of Impact Leaders. These are people who accept their freedom to take personal initiative to make a difference that matters.

To sustain a culture that is marked by trust and personal initiative requires a structure that is aligned for impact. The third piece of our alignment picture follows in the next chapter.

CHAPTER 9 QUESTIONS

The Relationship Dimension—
Creating Trusting Relationships

1. List five people in your organization whom you trust. List five people who trust you. Thank them for being trust-worthy people.

2. Describe the relationship culture in your organization. What one thing can you do to advance it towards being a stronger culture of trust?

3. What is one aspect of the relationship culture in your organization that you would like to improve over the next three months? How can you take personal initiative to impact that need?

10

THE STRUCTURE DIMENSION–
CREATING IMPACT
THAT MATTERS

One of the great underappreciated developments of the last century is the multinational corporate organizational structure. Imagine coordinating the work of tens of thousands of people around the world towards a common goal. It is a work of modern genius. The magnitude of this development is worth reflecting upon.

Three hundred years ago, most global organizations were expressions of colonial expansion of nation states. Expeditions ventured forth from the capital cities of Europe to discover the unknown. Once they left, they were on their own. There was no system of communication that stretched around the globe. It could be years before they were heard from. As they journeyed, they would meet tribal peoples who were still primitive in how they lived. Extreme poverty, illiteracy, and a short life span were the norm. Now, in the first decades of the 21st century, we are close to eradicating extreme poverty, education rates are rising worldwide, and scientists are talking about people regularly living past one hundred years old. It is an amazing age that we live in.

Today an organization of almost any size can extend its reach around the world with instantaneous communication and next-day delivery of goods. This was not imaginable a half century ago. The world is growing smaller. Travel between nations is easier than ever. Collaboration among people of different nationalities is a normal part of our lives.

A decade ago I collaborated on an e-book on morale in the workplace with people from twelve countries on four continents. The conversation that formed the content of the book showed that our common experience is greater than the differences of our national cultures. People are people, regardless of where they call home. The places where my friends and family live outside the United States are now places of local concern to me. It isn't really that the world is shrinking, but that our perception of life has changed.

It is tempting to think that the changes that we are experiencing are just us becoming a more global society. That is part of the story, but a more important one is worth telling. There is another kind of change that marks the real transition from the 20th to the 21st century.

Two Global Forces of Change

Think about the transition that we are experiencing as the product of an increasing capacity of people and organizations to do more, reach further, and solve problems that have been present for millennia. This historic moment of transition is represented by two global trends. One is older, more institutional, now reaching its apex, the other is just emerging to become the guiding trend for the future. I described these two forces of change earlier as between structures of centralized control and decentralized networks of relationships.

The older force of change is that of global institutions of governance and finance. These are the organizations that were created in the aftermath of two world wars to promote prosperity and peace in the world. These global organizations came into being because world leaders lacked the confidence that their nations could, on their own, create a peaceful, prosperous world.

The other force of change is found in networks of relationships, where personal initiative for impact finds its best expression. The emergence of digital technology is a key element in the capacity of you and me, and billions of people around the world, to interact in ways that advance our shared commitment to making a difference in the world. Today, national and geographic boundaries are no longer obstacles to our individual desires to also bring peace and prosperity to the world.

The interaction between these two forces is a historic moment of transition. It is important that we understand why this transition is taking place.

The Force of Global Integration

For the past century, integrating national efforts for peace and prosperity into global organizations has been an ongoing process. The aim is to integrate as many functions of society into a seamless efficient system operating through global institutions of governance and finance.

As these organizations grew larger and more expansive, their connection to people in the localness of their lives became more distant. The larger the organization, the more difficult to recognize the individual differences that distinguish people, communities, or nations. Whether intentional or not, the system's impetus is towards a one-size-fits-all approach to the solution of problems. As a system of development, it succeeded in places where local cultures were ready.

The limitation of these organizations is in their hierarchical nature. Whether the hierarchy serves a thousand people or seven billion, all hierarchies are dependent on a small group of leaders to have the knowledge, the skills, the wisdom, and the character to make decisions that are in the best interest of the constituencies they serve. For several millennia hierarchical structure has defined the nature of leadership, where we find a few leaders ruling over their many subjects. The inherent weakness of hierarchy is that it is only as strong as the wisdom and character of the senior leader.

Hierarchy requires order to succeed. To create order on a large scale requires a structure for control over the hundreds or thousands of people under its leadership. To release control creates an opening for individual initiative and collaboration. This is the transition point that modern organizations have been passing through for at least a generation. The world we are living in today is one where the knowledge, skills, tools, and, to a certain extent, the resources for personal initiative, have become available to everyone. Today, institutional control over all the facets under your authority has become more difficult and less certain as the opinions of people through social media can overnight cause the termination of a leader or prominent cultural figure. This loss of control is a mark of a transition that is irreversible in my opinion.

The Force of Personal Initiative

The second force of change is reflected in the native desire of individuals on a global scale to live lives and do work that matters to them and for their communities. Their acts of human initiative operate within the context of relationships of trust and mutuality. The difference between these relationships and those within the institutions of global governance and finance is that these networks of relationships have no institutional mandate. Their relationships are free to form, to grow for a season, and then to recede or disband as other relationships emerge to take their place.

For many of us, these relationships originate online through social media platforms. We gather around common values, shared experiences and perspectives about life and work that transcend our national and cultural boundaries. This is my own experience as a global citizen. It is not that we rally to a global cause, but rather we move toward people and opportunities where our desire to be persons of impact can be realized.

These global networks of relationships are possible because the technology of handheld devices makes it possible to communicate with anyone anywhere there is a Wi-Fi connection. The obstacles to having personal impact in the lives of people globally have been reduced to a minimum. Networks of relationships, as a result, thrive in the context of interaction where we can contribute to one another's lives.

A core principle of the Circle of Impact is that all leadership begins with personal initiative. Its purpose is to create impact for the benefit of our local communities. Looking at this idea in the context of the relationships that social media fosters today, it is apparent that we are only in the first stages of recognizing the value of having boundary-free global relationships. I am convinced that this is because we are also in the first stages of people beginning to see that their lives can be defined by their actions, rather than by their association to an ideology or movement.

Chinese artist and activist Ai Weiwei aptly describes this perspective of living today. *"Your own acts tell the world who you are and what kind of society you think it should be."* This is the transition that is taking place which is entering us into a world far different than the one our parents and grandparents knew. Through the power of digital technology to connect us together, we can find the advice, the resources, and the motivation that we need to initiate positive change in the world.

Many of our acts of personal initiative are done without recognition.

- The gift of a meal to a hungry person.
- The mentoring that takes place in schools, sports, and in youth club programs.
- The volunteering that takes place in local communities through religious congregations and community nonprofits.
- Entrepreneurial programs to train and develop the leadership of new businesses.
- Event planners and consultants who bring people together to raise financial support for local programs.

- Meetings over coffee where community understanding and healing can begin to take place.

In each situation, it starts with a person taking initiative. Then it grows through the networks of relationships that emerge at both the local and global level.

For organizations, small and large, local or global, the character of people is becoming a leadership differentiator. When we take leadership initiative to solve a problem, to collaborate across institutional boundaries or create new processes of work, we are taking action to create a better future. When an organization encourages and creates the space for people to take personal initiative, a release of energy and productivity takes place. The potential hidden in people can be tapped into to advance a business. Instead of leadership being a top-down role within the structure of the organization, this is where a bottom-up culture of leadership grows to define the company or a community.

We are in the midst of a great transition as a global society. The hierarchical nature of global society that has existed for many millennia is changing to one where each of us can be persons of impact as leaders both in our local communities and through our relationships with people globally.

A Global Leadership Transition: Serge's Story

Our conversation began with an email, then a couple of Skype calls. Serge is a mid-level development officer for a global NGO (Non-government Organization) in one of the central African nations. He spends most of his days working with men and women in local villages on water projects.

Serge had seen the diagrams of the Circle of Impact online. He had questions about how the idea of personal initiative and networks of relationships could work in his context. As we talked, I realized that Serge was a transitional leader in his organization. He did not exactly agree with how things were managed. His issues were not with the people that he worked with in the villages, but with how his organization operated. There was a territorial pride within the organization. As a result, they only collaborated when they could be in charge. Serge saw things differently. He was focused on the impact that his water projects could bring to remote villages. If another NGO could help, he was all for it.

From the perspective of the Circle of Impact, the problem that Serge described was a conflict between the purpose of the organization as defined by its structure and its purpose as defined by the impact it sought to create. They were not so much in conflict but disconnected. The NGO was dependent upon people like Serge, who was comfortable taking personal initiative when needed. Our conversations focused on how Serge could work within the confines of his job while taking initiative to reach out beyond his NGO to find solutions for the projects he directed.

Serge was successful in his development work because he approached it as a problem that the network of the village needed to resolve. He was a facilitator and a resource person to the leaders of the villages in the region. Serge was effective because he was able to manage the inherent conflicts that existed between his role as a staff person with the agency and his ability to work with people to facilitate their growth as leaders.

Global Forces in Transition

Serge's story illustrates the tension that this transition is bringing to older, legacy institutions that have rested in their prominence. The emergence of networks of relationships that rise up to focus on a specific issue or opportunity is unique in human history. No governing authority must grant permission for a group of people to join together to address a need. This development became crystal-clear to me during the recovery efforts after Hurricane Katrina in 2005. I saw and experienced on several trips to the Mississippi Gulf Coast people from across the United States who had packed their bags, locked up their houses, and moved there to help. They showed up on their own initiative. I've observed this to be true in every natural disaster since. What these events also show is that the tension between older institutions of control and these new networks of relationships is the transition point that we need to pass through.

The relationship between hierarchical organizations and networks of relationships does not have to be an antagonistic one. They need one another. Global organizations need the vitality and adaptive capacity of the networks. And, networks need a structure where their impact can find a way to be sustained and replicated in other places. The challenge is one of perception of purpose and value, and the capacity to change how we are organized to meet the need as it exists in the present.

Global institutions of governance and finance are structured hierarchically. Leadership is an organizational role with institutional authority. This has been the nature of leadership for centuries. Human identity is established by its

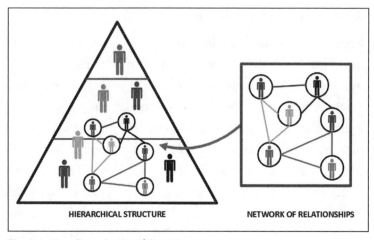

Figure 4: Two Organizational Structures

relationship to the hierarchical structure of order. We know one another as members of this tribe, nation, or organization. The advent of individual self-perception is a recent development in human history.

In a hierarchical structure, impact, or whatever is the product of the structure, is produced through delegated responsibility based on the specific organizational role a person performs. Authority is derived from one's place in the structure. Leadership is a top-down function of direction and control. Individual responsibility is delegated and managed up through the structure of managers. The organization's purpose is internally focused on the maintenance of the integrity of the organization. All aspects of the organization serve that purpose. In times of gradual change, the modern hierarchical organization has provided social stability and economic prosperity wherever it has been developed with ethical integrity.

Global networks of relationships are structured through relationships of social trust. There is no role of leader in a network of relationships. A person may convene or facilitate the formation and conduct of a network. Leadership is exercised as the shared responsibility within the network. It is leadership by the first-among-equals, as Robert Greenleaf, author of *The Servant as Leader*, has described. The person with the specific knowledge, experience, or expertise takes the lead. Authority comes from the trust earned in relationship with the other members of the network.

In a network structure, social trust establishes the authenticity of the person. The purpose of the network is not its own integrity, but rather the impact that can be created through the network. It has come into being because some external need or opportunity has brought people together. The structure is meant to serve the organization's purpose for impact.

In an organizational structure, a network tends to exist for a specific purpose and for a defined period of time. They exist for as long as there is a reason why they have been brought together. Outside of formal institutional structures, networks of relationships provide people connections to ideas, resources, and organizational support as a function of relationships of trust. It is not beyond reason to characterize these relationships as professional friendships in the richest sense of the term.

This transition in global structures presents traditional hierarchical organizations a challenging opportunity. The transition is too far along to think that they can simply ignore the emergence of human initiative that functions outside of their control. The emergence of global networks of relationships, while in its early stages of development, is touching a desire in people to be connected and engaged in making a difference in the world together. This transition has been carried along by digital technology and the social environment of the internet. While we need to understand the distinction between hierarchical structures and networks of relationships, we also need to understand that these networks are different than what takes places through social media. The difference is critical to understand.

The Difference between Social Media and Networking

It would seem that the creation of networks of relationships would be the most natural thing because people are so involved with social media. Unfortunately, this not the case. Our human involvement in social media is about the projection of our individual voice into a large arena filled to standing room only. There is mostly noise, and occasionally someone's voice gets heard over the din of sound. In a network, we speak and listen, lead and follow, as we join together seeking a shared goal. The only true similarity is that there are people involved.

There is a science to these networks that makes it possible for them to work inside of traditional organizational structures. One of the images of these networks is of a hub-and-spoke design. A person who is a hub in a network is one who has connections to people that other people do not have. The hub brings people together to form a circle of relationships. The hub of the network is the connector, but not necessarily the leader. The hub creates an environment of trust where people can take personal initiative with the others to create a shared impact.

Several years ago, the e-book that I created on morale in the workplace was for the purpose of a training program for a group of young managers of a large company. In this situation, as the convener and facilitator of the discussion, I was the hub of the network. I asked the questions that prompted others to comment. I would respond to comments with questions that extended the thought process for the group. Our group of thirty-six people from twelve countries on four continents produced a conversation of significant insight and perspective for my training program. With the assistance of one of the members of our network, the e-book was produced for the participants and other members of our online leadership community.

A network structure provides each of us a place for the personal and social aspects of our lives to find expression. When we establish a relationship with a person who is a network hub, we are taking personal initiative to establish a relationship with the hub and their network. If we enter the relationship with this person seeking their assistance, we look to connect with people who can join us in an effort focused on a particular purpose for impact.

If we go to a hub seeking connection, we may say something like, *"Knowing what I'm interested in, who do you know that you believe that I should know? Will you make an introduction for me?"* Using this approach, I have developed relationships with people who have become valued colleagues and friends. This is a basic strategy for networking. Be a hub by nurturing relationships of shared trust and purpose. Be a spoke by contributing to the network through personal initiative to create impact.

The essential difference between networking and social media is the relationship component. In the network, the relationship is the focus. Our participation on social media is to make connections for social positioning. Clicking "like" or sending an emoji may or may not have any relational impact. The connectional nature of social media, though, can provide a place to begin a relationship. You have to be intentional in this regard. For me, there are many people that I met through social media that I have taken the initiative to meet in person. There is no substitute for having a real face-to-face conversation with a person.

The opportunities for networking are right there on the social media platforms. However, they're not happening for two reasons.

First, to create a network of relationships requires intention and effort. It does not happen automatically. Relationships don't form because we express an opinion. We form relationships because we show interest in another person. A network forms one relationship at a time. A large network can form quickly when a person that we know invites his network to support our idea or cause. Even then, those are not relationships, but social connections that can be mobilized to make a difference that matters. Direct relationships require effort to create and maintain. Social media does not require this.

Social media is a platform for social posturing. The activity is limited to posting, sharing, clicking "like," or commenting. It is about attracting attention by posting an opinion. If a relationship forms as a result of an encounter through a social media platform, then it still requires one-to-one effort to make the relationship work.

Second, social media doesn't function like a network. The purpose is not to form a network of relationships. Though it could happen with intention and hard work. Social media platforms are marketing platforms. Some people and companies market to sell products. Others market to influence opinion. Even if the social media platform is used for a social or political cause, it is still a platform for sharing information and opinion. My point here is that we should not be confused by thinking that the energy we give to social media is equivalent to that which we give to establishing networks of relationships. They are not the same.

Being a Circle of Impact Leader, who takes personal initiative to create impact that makes a difference that matters, requires that we align our lives with the three dimensions of leadership. We need to be clear about our values and our purpose for impact. We need to be willing to do the work of building trusting relationships. And, we need to be willing to establish networks of relationships that allow us to scale the impact that we desire to create. Leadership is both personal and social. This is what Brian brought to the nonprofit organization that he was hired to lead.

Transitioning to a Network Structure: Brian's Story

Brian didn't accept the executive director's job with the nonprofit organization so that he could be a boss. He accepted because he wanted to lead a team. The problem was the organization had been run as a top-down, hands-off, transactional relationship organization for a long time. The former director had his favorites on the staff. They correctly realized that Brian was going to be a different leader. So, they sought to remove him before he could change anything. Because Brian was a leader of proven character and awareness, he was able to manage this initial crisis in his tenure as executive director.

The challenge was changing the culture. It is one thing to be clear about your values. It is another thing to be able to build trust with your staff. Ultimately, you have to lead the organization. The structure of the organization was poorly suited for the growth that the board envisioned, and why they hired Brian.

While he was the senior executive of the organization, and each program director reported to him, he wanted his team to be a real team. This meant that he had to make structural changes. He did this over time, in conversation with each of his program directors. The result was a hub-and-spoke program structure. Each program would be treated equally, unlike their previous management. The program directors would function as an executive team. To facilitate the equality of each of the programs, and the mutual support of all the programs, Brian rotated the facilitator of this group on a monthly basis. They designed their team meetings to focus on the strategic growth of the program, and to be a committee of the whole in addressing strategic problem situations in each of the programs. Brian served as an ex officio member with the right to veto any major strategic change or expenditure. He would bring strategic initiatives to the group for its consideration.

Implementing a network structure of rotating leadership changed the culture of the organization. Every problematic situation, instead of bringing out resistance and defensiveness, was viewed as an opportunity to create impact in a new way. He accomplished this because he built a team who owned the programs and the whole of the organization. Their shared leadership for impact changed the culture of sports in their city.

The Future Is Relational

All my life I have watched, observed, listened, checked my assumptions, changed my mind, and ended up with few thoughts of which I'm certain. Here are three that I am.

The first thought is that we are all in transition.

I'm convinced that the transition that we are in now is at a level unseen in a very long time. The advance of digital technology gives us the power to create change that has never existed in human history. Our future is tied to what you and I decide it will be. The development of technology is an advance, but I'm also convinced that it is not our destiny. We have a choice about the future we want.

The second thought that I'm certain about is that the way we organize and order the world will look very different than it has the past hundred years. I do not see large, centralized global institutions as sustainable financially or rationally from a perspective of their impact. They serve a valuable purpose, and like other institutional forms, will change or fade into irrelevance. This isn't a judgment of their mission, but rather a recognition of the place of organizational structures for the future. Which leads to my third conclusion.

I'm convinced that the future belongs to people who are able to forge high-quality networks of relationships. These relationships are not contractual ones. They are instead relationships of shared purpose, energized by shared values, and with a vision for impact. The relational character of these networks means that being persons of authentic character will be the measure of trust. In this sense the future will be more intensely and critically personal and social.

This perspective that has led me to create the Circle of Impact model of leadership. Align your life and your business with the three dimensions of leadership, and I believe that you will be able to balance the need to change with the need to create a stable, sustainable way to live and work. In an environment of constant change, the Circle of Impact provides a platform for managing the changes in perception, relationship, and structure that will be constantly present.

While the Circle of Impact provides a simple, practical tool for leaders and their organizations, it is important to understand it in the context of our world in transition. Section four will guide us through this perspective.

The Structure Dimension— Creating Sustainable Impact

1. What is the most pressing issue that you are facing in your organization? Write it down.

2. Of the three dimensions of leadership—ideas, relationships, or organizational structure—which is the one that your pressing need is about?

3. If you were to resolve your most pressing issue today, what is the impact that you would like to see as a result?

PART FOUR

LEADERSHIP IMPACT FOR A WORLD IN TRANSITION

11

LEADING AS CREATORS
OF CHANGE

When I began my consulting practice in the mid-1990s, the world was a very healthy, stable place. A decade later terrorism and a global economic recession brought chaos and war to the world. I was impacted just like many people.

"We are not going to be able to work with you. The project is on hold.... Sorry, we were looking forward to working with you again." This message, followed by five similar calls in successive weeks, alerted me that the context of my business had changed. It wasn't the first time that this had happened. This time was different. It wasn't just a simple drop-off of business for a few months. These were the endings to business relationships.

During those years of change, a troubling pattern revealed itself to me. The reason my projects would not go forward implied an approach to change that I felt was mistaken. The unexpressed assumption was that all an organization needed to do to manage change was to cut back on costs and wait for better times to return. Change was just an irritant, a little stone in my shoe. Remove the stone and things would go back to normal.

The conventional attitude was, *"We'll wait for conditions to improve. It worked in the past. It will do so again."* I felt that this was a far too passive approach for the kind of change we were experiencing. We had entered a time of transition globally that was not an accident of the marketplace or of a natural disaster. It was the outcome of structural changes being made in businesses and governments worldwide. This kind of change required a more deliberate, intentional response. We were now in a time where the pain of not changing had become greater than the pain of changing.

The Circle of Impact guides my assessment of changing circumstances. The changes I saw were not downturns in performance, but a fundamental restructuring taking place in the world. This perspective is captured in the idea, described earlier, that there are two global forces pushing and pulling against one another. The push was to centralize the management of finance and government on a global scale. The pull was to decentralize the structures of daily life and work into networks of relationships. This was a change that called us to leave a passive belief that there was a natural state of what is normal and stable.

If we look back over time, we'll see that human history has always been the story of change. The difference, say, between a half century ago and today is the speed and extent of the change that affects our daily lives. Then, traditional human values guided change. Today, technological advancement does. We live at a transition point in human history where change has moved from small incremental steps over the course of centuries to revolutionary change in the matter of months or years. It is not for this reason alone that I believe we must become creators of change.

Becoming a Change Creator

Being a change creator is a mindset utilizing a specific skill set focused on impact. Instead of asking, *"What does it take to create a happy customer?"* ask, *"What is the impact that we want to create for our customer?"* When we have a change mindset, we see difference. We see how what we do creates that difference. We communicate that difference so that we can strengthen our relationship with customers. We change to adapt ourselves to the needs of our customer. By recognizing this changing difference, we begin to grasp that we are always in transition. Terry's story shows us how.

Listening for Change: Terry's Story

Terry had a wholesale sports apparel business. He supplied mostly small specialty stores with apparel that aligned with their markets. An economic downturn hit Terry's business as customers cut back on orders or closed their accounts completely. Terry had unsold inventory without an easy way to sell it. He started his change process by opening a small shop catering to students from the nearby university. Within a few weeks, his inventory was not just sold, but had totally turned over into apparel lines that he had never sold in the past.

While students were the initial buyers of his inventory, it was young professional women who became his new market niche. These women first came in looking for sportswear.

However, they talked to Terry about their need for inexpensive fashion-conscious clothes. Terry discovered that there were a number of small manufacturers who were developing popular designs in limited numbers. Terry decided to try something similar. He rented more space and began to market a limited inventory of cutting-edge designs from the companies his female customers said they liked. Each selection, offered in limited numbers and sizes, and not to be reordered, would sell out. The phenomenon of the passive shopper changed to one of the opportunistic one.

Terry discovered a market niche that was insufficiently served. He listened to the women who came into his shop. They too had been impacted by the recession. While their incomes dropped, the pressure to compete in a changing environment increased. Terry provided them fashionable inexpensive clothing in limited numbers. As a result, Terry had a steady stream of customers turning what had been a common inventory problem into an asset.

Terry's story is an example of how the Circle of Impact shows us how to address issues of change. His problem was that the wholesale structure of his business no longer worked. He created a retail shop, just as a temporary measure until he figured out a better plan. Terry's mindset was to listen to his customers to find new opportunities to serve them. His response to his new women customers led him to repurpose his business with an innovative approach to retail merchandising.

Was Terry just in the right place at the right time to discover a new market? Or was Terry prepared to change because he understood how to align the three dimensions of leadership within his business? For many of us, it is not so easy. We are trapped by the way we have always worked and the structure of the businesses where it takes place. Everything is so predictable we don't even see change happening until it becomes a painful, disruptive experience.

With a changed mindset, we need a skill set to move from a reactive, resistance stance to a more proactive, opportunistic one.

Seeing the Context of Change

It is vitally important that we understand what change is. It is the living, dynamic context of our lives. Every thought, every emotion, every action, every response in a particular moment operates within a change context. Every movement, shift in perspective, or initiative taken happens within the context of change.

Change is so prevalent that we don't even see it. It is invisible until it becomes toxic or threatening. Then, we see it or feel it so much that we want to get out of it. Change is always present. It is our best friend and our worst enemy.

The skill needed is a recognition that we are always in transition. It is not just a mental note that change is always present. It is seeing precisely what kind of change is happening in the moment. Did I anticipate my clients stepping back from the projects we had planned? I was not surprised. All around me were people I knew whose businesses were in crisis. Did Terry anticipate his customers closing their accounts with him? His response suggests that he was always aware that change was possible.

Seeing the context of change that we are in is a macro picture of change. We see change as always present with us. This leads to the second skill that we need as creators of change. Situational awareness is the micro picture of change.

Situational Awareness

To see the context of change is to recognize that we are always in it. Change is always with us. Every situation we walk into is a context of change. Every phone call. Every meeting. Every report we write or read. Every contract we create and sign. Every employee we hire. Everyone we terminate. Every aspect of what we do every day is operating within the context of change. Within each of those contexts of change are possibilities of change that demand that we develop the skill of situational awareness.

Imagine what that moment was like when Terry realized that these young professional women were offering him an opportunity to develop a new network of clients. That singular moment could have easily passed by if all he was thinking about was liquidating his sports apparel inventory. But that isn't Terry. He saw in each encounter with a customer a range of possibilities that could produce a beneficial impact for the customer and for him.

The initial moment occurred for Terry when a young woman, who was in the shop to purchase a tennis skirt, asked about a particular dress designer. Instead of saying that he didn't know, he said, *"I'll find out, and get back to you."* He contacted the designer's company. He asked if he could get a sample of dresses, and from that moment on his new business grew.

Being situationally aware within the context of change requires us to put aside our fear of change, our desire to remain comfortable, and our lack of confidence so that we can stretch ourselves into new areas of our lives and work. Instead of being focused on what is internally going on within us, we focus outwardly to see every situation as an opportunity to make a difference.

Being situationally aware means that we have a framework, a mindset, that helps us interpret what we see happening. This is why it is important for us to be clear about our purpose, our values, and the kind of impact that we want to create. These ideas frame our vision for what to look for in our interactions with people. When we are clear, our capacity for having an impact with people in social situations becomes simpler. We don't have to stand there wondering about what we are supposed to do. Instead, we know the kind of impact that we want to create in that moment. We become creators of change as persons of impact.

Being situationally aware in the context of change is being ourselves on demand. Situational awareness means that we are looking for opportunities, not to just do anything, but the one thing that fulfills our sense of purpose for impact.

The opportunity may be an unmet need like the one Terry discovered. Or maybe it is a conflict that occurs between two people. Or maybe it is a solution to a badly managed client crisis. Whatever the situation presents, we are aware that we can make a difference. In many of these cases, we don't have the answer, but we know the person who does. So, we make a connection that changes how that situation unfolds.

If we decide to live lives that are to make a difference that matters, it means that the context of change is a place of creativity, not resistance. The opportunities that await us come from seeing them in the moment-to-moment experience of living. The context of change is not just a place of disruption and disorientation. It is where we discover our true potential through the actions we take.

To create change is to create impact. When we do, we are bringing the three dimensions of leadership into alignment. There is a simplicity that results when the Circle of Impact moves from being an abstract diagram to a concrete intuitive awareness of how we can make a difference in the moment of opportunity. The benefit to us is that this makes us more agile and responsive in situations that in the past may have paralyzed us with fear or self-doubt.

The Speed of Change

Just as change takes place within a context, it also happens in time. It is here that we feel the effects of change that is not a product of our actions. The third skill set we need is how to operate in a change context that is rapidly changing.

Many people want to slow change down. They feel that they need time to adapt, to accommodate themselves to a new situation. I've learned that the more time you have to change, the more time we have for feelings of fear, anxiety, and self-doubt to grow. We begin to question our decisions, our motivations, and even our perception of what we see. By trying to slow change down, we end up making a change process even more complicated than it already is.

If Terry had overthought whether he should venture into the women's apparel retail business, he could have missed out on a market that was looking for someone to fulfill it. It isn't that there is no thought given to change. Rather, there is only so much thinking that can be done to determine if a decision is the right one or not. In fact, I have seen so many situations where overthinking a decision leads the person or organization to lose perspective.

A loss of perspective is forgetting why we do what we do. Instead of being focused on the positive outcome of our impact, we become worried about a negative one. If we let fear govern our decisions, we will lose confidence. Most of our issues with change are not about the change itself, but our insecurity over whether we can follow through effectively on our decisions. When we overthink, we believe the perfect plan will give us the confidence that we need. It can just as easily lead us to decision paralysis.

Confidence in the midst of the change comes not from our inner motivation to overcome all obstacles. It comes from the experience of making decisions and successfully following through on them. In other words, self-confidence comes from creating change that fulfills our purpose for impact.

This is why the Circle of Impact can provide the foundation for perspective and action. When we align the four connecting ideas into a single vision of the impact we want to achieve, we gain a focus that we need to carry us through multiple transition points and the decisions that are necessary. To be clear about our purpose for impact simplifies our perspective. We are not worried about whether we are making the right decision. Rather, we act with confidence, based on our purpose, and if we need to decide and act multiple times in a short period of time, we can do it with assurance.

Still, it is difficult to grasp the idea that the faster we change, the slower the process feels. I have come to understand it in this way: When we delay making a decision, we have every good intention of being comprehensive, covering all our bases, and being thorough in our due diligence. There are many decision areas where this is advisable, as in a major financial decision. But most of our decisions do not require an absolute, airtight argument for us to decide to move forward. Instead, in many cases, there is no way to know until we have taken action whether our decision is the right one.

I have found that when we spend an inordinate amount of time thinking through a change process we tend not to become clearer in our perspective, but more indecisive. Doubt grows as a result. I say this as a person who is prone to being a perfectionist in preparing for change. I've learned that few of these change decisions are absolute. They are situations in the moment that the next decision can correct or advance.

When we know that we must change, we should act as soon as possible. For within a relatively short period of time, another set of decisions will be presented to us. By acting and moving on, we shift from seeking perfect answers to becoming masters of adapting to changing circumstances. The strength of learning to adapt to the speed of change is agility.

With agility, we begin to see how the transitions that we experience begin to flow together. A continuity of change begins to form in our awareness. As a result, we begin to discover that which we thought we had lost as disruptive change began to affect us. The flow of change brings confidence, and the always readiness to take initiative to create impact.

When we act as soon as we know we must change, then we remove those time periods of anxiety, fear, and self-doubt. We move from one decision to the next with ever-growing confidence. Without those conflicting emotions, time smooths out and seems to slow in its pace.

The Call to Create Change

My first encounter with leadership impact came when I joined the Midtown Alliance Board of Directors in Atlanta, Georgia, in the mid-1980s. For the first time in my life, I found contributors, collaborators, communicators, and creators of impact. The influence of these men and women on me as a young man inspired me to focus my life's work on leadership that creates impact.

The Circle of Impact is as much a model for creating change as it is a leadership model. In reality, the two arenas go hand in hand. Without change, there is no leadership, and without leadership, change becomes a disruptive, disorienting experience.

The question that many people have is, *"How do I change my life? How do I discover what I need to do to be a creator of change?"* At the end of this chapter is a set of questions that I recommend people use to help them identify how to create a life of leadership impact. I call them The Five Impact Questions. They are best used when we regularly ask them. For example, spend fifteen minutes every week asking these questions. Over time, you will find that your perception of how you spend your time and what you want from it will change. You'll find a sense of purpose growing within you. You'll discover an awareness of what is taking place in and around your life that has been missing. You may find that where you are in your work is at a transition point. It may be time for you to make a personal change that takes you in a new direction.

My advice is that, as you use the five questions, you enter each session with an open mind, and that you keep a record of the answers that you have. The first time you ask the questions, spend only five minutes. Answer them quickly. Then come back a day or two later and spend a longer period of time. The reason for this is to jump-start your mind and emotions to become sensitive to these questions as you go through your daily experience. When you sit down to spend more time answering the questions, you will be prepared to reflect more deeply on their meaning.

This process of asking questions and applying the Circle of Impact serves as a call to action to become a person who makes a difference that matters.

The Five Impact Questions

1. What has changed in my life and work? How am I in transition?

   a. How am I in transition right now from where I was in the past to where I will be in the future?

   b. What has changed about my self-perception, my relationships, and the structure of my life and work?

2. What is my impact?

   a. What is the impact I'm having right now with my ideas, through my relationships, and in the structure of my life and work?

   b. What is the difference that matters that I want to make in the future?

3. Who am I impacting?

   a. Who is being most significantly impacted by me and what I am doing right now?

   b. How can I expand the impact that I'm having on those people?

4. What opportunities do I have now?

   a. What opportunities do I have because of the impact that I am making?

   b. Which of those opportunities do I need to take action on right now?

5. What problems have I created? What obstacles do I face?

   a. What problems or obstacles that I have right now keep me from taking advantage of my opportunities to take personal initiative to create impact?

   b. Which problem or obstacle is most critical for resolving immediately?

   c. How am I going to create a change process to resolve it?

(12)

CREATING A CULTURE
FOR LEADERSHIP

What happens when the past is no longer an accurate predictor of the future? Some of us cling more closely to the proven ways of past, resisting the future as a threat to the security that we have built. Then there are people who opportunistically play a different kind of game. They defend the past hoping that it is sustainable into the future. They do so even as they plan to take advantage of the changes that they see coming. Their rationale is that the past is known and is more certain, secure, stable, and comfortable—until it isn't. Their game of finesse, playing the future off against the past, is no more predictable than the person firmly rooted in the past.

Our world is in the midst of a historic transition. For some people, their past success is an obstacle to future success. They cannot see beyond their own past experience to what might be possible in the future. They continue to approach problems and the function of their businesses as they always have. Their once strong position erodes as their once privileged position makes it hard to adapt to the changes taking place. They wonder what went wrong, looking to blame others or society at large because they cannot see how their choices are the source of their failures.

Many of us are experiencing this transitional point in history as disruptive and disorienting. The social and organizational structures that we have depended upon for strength and stability over the past century no longer seem so stable. We hear world leaders lamenting the end of world order because they can't see that they, too, are in transition. Like many, they cannot see that the signs of change are also ones of opportunity.

It is a particular mark of this transition that our vision of the future is so dependent upon seeing the past as a predictor of the future. I saw this in particular during the global recession at the end of the first decade of the 2000's. People could not see the event as a transition to a new era. It was only a painful time to endure. Our view of the future is far more retrospective than prospective. We can imagine what we want for the future, only as a reflection of what we've had or not had in the past. However, if we can't see that the conditions for our lives and organizations are changing, then the path forward is unclear.

When I speak about structure-centric organizations of change, this is what I see. The resistance to change makes it hard for us to see the tension between the two global forces of centralization and decentralization, as described in chapters six and ten, as a key to understanding the future. By not seeing that the growing opportunities for personal initiative to make a difference are not dependent upon the dominant structures of the past, is to end up becoming prisoner of our past decisions.

Then there are those who never found success in the past, and for whom the changes that are taking place are felt as liberation to a new world of opportunity. They use all the new tools of the digital age to build networks of relationships and enterprise that are not dependent upon historic structures. For them, the chaos of change that the world is experiencing is fuel for building a future of success that was never possible for them before.

To see change as a transition is to also understand where this transition is taking us. Time is no longer a luxury. Long arcs of development become more problematic. As a result, we each need to be agile and open to taking advantage of the opportunities of the moment. As soon as the change we should make becomes clear, we must take the initiative to do so. This transition begins with a change in our own self-perception. To embrace the future that is emerging is to accept that each of us can become persons of leadership impact right now.

For example, no one really believes in heroic leadership anymore. We no longer expect our leaders to be all-knowing, wise, and decisive in battle. Instead, we are satisfied if our leaders are simply honest and hardworking, not making dumb mistakes that make our lives more difficult. It is not that we just know more now about society's leaders. Instead, and more importantly, it is that the world changed and the kind of leadership that we celebrated in the past is no longer adequate to the challenges we face.

In the not too distant past, everyone's relationship to an organization was mediated through its structure. Titles and departmental structures determined what you did and who you could talk to, and businesses operated in a straightforward way. Everyone knew their place and the delegated expectations that came with their role. Enter the information age and the computer, and now the smartphone and the cloud, which are changing how organizations function. They are less structured in the traditional sense, and more open and relational. A premium is now placed on the skills of human interaction. Personal interaction is replacing the formality of structural boundaries. How many leaders were prepared for this?

Where once the structure of an organization dictated a relationship of followers to their leader, now networks of leadership initiators are changing organizations. As a result, the possibilities for an individual to make a difference in life are growing.

Releasing Hidden Human Potential

Over the past half century, much of the leadership literature has been filled with simple, inspirational ideas that provide tactical advice for improving organizations. The problem is that too often simple ideas are not practical. They may have an inspirational quality to them, but at the same time they lack a sense of reality. When I describe leadership as beginning with personal initiative, it is a simple idea that may not be very clear, but I can make it inspirational. Complex ideas, on the other hand, require engagement in real situations to understand. In our changing self-perception, we need to see that we are already learning to master these complex situations.

If I say, *"Leaders take initiative to create impact with ideas, through relationships and within social and organizational structures,"* I'm presenting a more complex idea that may cause you to stop and think for a moment. This description of Circle of Impact Leadership challenges us to look beyond what is simplistic and superficial to an underlying reality that we already know. Simple ideas validate our perception of the world when we feel insecure. Complex ideas challenge us to look more deeply into why things are the way they are, and how to work within that complexity. We can work through these situations to discover simple, practical ideas that can guide our steps. We are already doing this every day. The Circle of Impact is a tool that can help us do it better.

When I say that being a leader is possible for every individual, regardless of who they are and their life situation, I am not being idealistic. I am speaking about what I already see. I see people already taking personal initiative to improve how their office functions. Others are transforming the way they relate to clients. All these hidden leaders may get no pat on the back or improved standing for doing this. They do it because it aligns with their values. They become Circle of Impact Leaders and their businesses and communities benefit because the structure works better.

Many of the businesses that I've worked with over the years have ways of measuring the efficiency of their processes. Few, if any, have ways of measuring the potential of their employees. When I ask them the question, *"What percentage of your employees' potential are you realizing?"* it isn't that they don't have an answer. They don't even know where to begin to find the answer. There is not a category of measurement defined as *"unrealized potential."* If it is not clear what the potential impact of your people is, then how do you know what the potential impact of your company is? Potential is a question of scale. How do you scale your business for impact? How do you scale the social culture of your business to free people to pursue the fulfillment of their potential impact? This is where we can begin to grasp a picture of the future that is not simply a replication of the past.

Who, Why, and How: Roberta's Story

Roberta is the executive director of a local nonprofit whose board is divided. Monthly board meetings are battle royales over everything. When we first met, the situation had been described to me by one of the board members as highly divisive. He was very frustrated by what he saw as the stubbornness of some of the other board members. I asked Roberta what her perspective was.

"It's all personal for them. They each have their reason for being here. They are extraordinarily caring people. But it is so personal to them that they cannot see what the other board members see." I asked if there were any members who were able to have a broader view. She just shook her head.

Roberta's board problem isn't simple. It is complex. Her problem is a toxic mix of each of the three dimensions. The ideas problem is that no consensus of the organization's values and purpose exists. The program structure is all there is. It serves as the public expression of board members' private agendas.

The relationship problem is that members of the board don't like one another. Some refuse to work together. They are there to press their issues and get their way. There is little respect for the other members and no trust among them.

The structural problem is a board structure problem. It is set up for conflict, not collaboration. Half the board does not want change, and the other half only wants change. Roberta sits in the middle. The board is in transition, as the two perspectives on change represent. Without clarity of values, and a culture of trust, the structure has no way of adapting to the changing circumstances that are taking place in their community which impact their mission.

This is not an unusual situation. In small and large businesses, professional practices, nonprofit boards, and local government agencies, the challenge of executive leadership is the problem of *who, why,* and *how.* In Roberta's situation, the board does not know *who* they are, *why* the board matters, or *how* they are to function in the best interest of the organization.

In overly complex organizational situations, complexity can produce personalism. By personalism, I am referring to when a person internalizes their involvement to focus on their individual interests. It simplifies the complex. But does it position the organization for impact?

Roberta defines her main problem as how to unify a board that cannot think beyond each member's own personal agenda. The complexity of her problem is that the board lacks alignment across the spectrum of the three dimensions of leadership. Each dimension, at the board level, is in crisis. She wants to know, *"Where do I start?"*

Roberta cannot solve her board problem until she can picture the entirety of her organization's problem culture. She needs a framework that can help her see the whole of her situation. The Circle of Impact model provides that perspective. For Roberta, she needs to begin with her own relationship to the organization and its board. As the executive leader, she must be clear about her values, her place in the structure, and her commitment to see this change process through.

Roberta needs to ask her own *who, why* and *how* questions:

- *Who is she as the executive director of this organization? Program director, change agent, board therapist?*

- *What is her real role within the organization? Not the role she was hired to do, but the role that emerges in the day-to-day realities of operating this organization.*

These questions address the dynamics of executive leadership in the 21st century. This kind of leadership is both personal and social. She needs to ask:

- *Why is she serving this organization? Does she have a personal commitment to her organization's mission or is this a job that she is skilled to do and glad to perform until a new opportunity comes along?*

- *Do the relationships that she has with the board, the staff, and the community give her hope that the current problems can be overcome? Or is there a social dysfunction operating here that cannot be resolved apart from disbanding the board and electing a new one?*

These questions begin to dig into the cultural fabric of the organization that seems to have been fraying for quite some time.

- *How is she going to lead an organization that is so dysfunctional? Where does she start? Which one of the three dimensions of leadership represents the most critical need for change?*

This question goes directly to the future of executive leadership. The purpose of aligning the three dimensions is to create a culture for leadership impact. A Circle of Impact culture is marked by clarity of purpose, trust among all the parties, and an agile organization structure focused on creating impact that matters. When that alignment is missing, current structural forms, based upon past leadership decisions, resist the consideration that is needed to find a pathway to impact. Structures don't resist change. People do. The structures represent their historic power and authority whose preservation has become the default purpose of the organization.

The chaos in Roberta's organization is a signal that the organization is in transition. Is it a choice between change or oblivion that is before them? Or do the people who continue to believe in the mission of the organization, who are outside the board, represent the future of the organization? This is the challenge that Roberta faces. It begins with her own self-perception as a leader. Is she just marking time until the next job comes along? Or does she have the desire and the vision to be a Circle of Impact Leader for this time of transition?

Becoming an Executive Leader: Linda's Story

Linda is the chief assistant to Sondra, the owner of a successful industry research group. According to Linda, and other staff members whom I interviewed, Sondra is a distracted, often absent owner/manager. Outside business and community interests occupy her time. The others see her as distracted from the challenges facing the research group. Linda has more of the day-to-day interaction with clients. She tells me that they want more engagement with Sondra as the leader of the company. Linda sees that the company is at a crossroads. There are opportunities to expand into new industries. The problem, as Linda sees it, is that Sondra is not focused enough to develop new client relationships.

During my interview with Linda, she tells me that she has had an initial conversation with Sondra about buying the company. Linda's husband has just sold his engineering firm. He is not ready to retire, so he is looking for something new to do. The idea of owning a technical research business appeals to him. As her assistant, Linda's husband could manage the company while she develops the relationships with current clients and takes steps to develop new clients.

The Circle of Impact is a guide for how a person like Linda can move from a staff position to an executive leadership role as owner. Each one of the three dimensions of leadership will change for Linda and the staff of the organization. Her self-perception changes from being one of the staff to being their boss. Their self-perception changes as they have to adjust to Linda's new role in the business.

Relationships between Linda and her staff will change. It will require Linda to be clear about what her expectations are for them. She knows them as a coworker, which may be a problem for some of them. They may feel that she knows things about them that places them at a disadvantage in their relationship with her as their boss. She needs to clearly communicate her expectations for their work.

Linda and her husband need to have a clear grasp on how the organization needs to function in the future, especially in those areas that needed improvement during Sondra's ownership. As a part of this restructuring of the business, Linda and her husband need to clarify the company's values and purpose for impact. This becomes their foundation for a Circle of Impact Leadership culture.

Every person who desires to achieve significance in their life and work must address the three dimensions of leadership. Both Roberta and Linda are facing challenging situations in their roles with their organizations. The challenge for Roberta is in aligning the organization as it goes through a long-needed transition. The challenge for Linda is to create a culture that allows the company to grow under her leadership.

Transitioning to a Leadership Culture?

Both Roberta's and Linda's organizations are in transition. Whatever they have been in the past is not going to be sufficient to address the complexity of operating a business in the future. They must shift to an impact focus as they develop a leadership-rich culture.

One of my first leadership roles was in a small community nonprofit that had languished for a decade and a half with little growth. My efforts to grow the organization were thwarted by a belief that the organization's golden years were in the past. The members looked back to a particular moment of decision that required a compromise with great pride and satisfaction. Instead of that moment being the start of growth, it established a level of operation that they never rose above.

Executive leaders are faced with a transition where one's managerial expertise may not be sufficient to lead the organization. New skills in creating a leadership culture are required.

The Circle of Impact model of leadership directs us toward what kind of culture is needed for leadership impact. All cultures are human cultures. They are created around the beliefs and practices of human beings. For an organization like the one I described, or like the ones that Roberta and Linda lead, it requires a change in self-perception on the part of the people involved.

More than likely, none were hired or joined with the expectation that they would be asked to become leaders of impact. Their initial perception is they were hired to do a job defined by a set range of tasks. And when each task is done, they can go home to the activities that they really enjoy. Human culture in modern organizations has developed as a kind virtual assembly line of managed activities. We do things asked of us because there is a social expectation that accompanies the job. This is not a leadership culture.

The Circle of Impact is a model for a leadership culture. It focuses each person on the impact that they desire to create. Relationships of trust grow as members of the company agree to work towards the achievement of their impact. Relationships of trust and cooperation grow out of the practice of shared values. Together, we design the kind of organizational structure needed to produce the impact that we seek. This is a picture of the alignment of the Circle of Impact.

The change in perception that happens when people are in a leadership impact culture is that they see themselves as Circle of Impact Leaders. Their lives become focused on the difference that they can make in their life and work. Their life is not focused on completing tasks on their calendar. They are focused on the change that results from each task and activity.

The creation of a Circle of Impact Leadership culture begins at the top of the organizational hierarchy. For if there is a disconnect between the executive team and the employees, the culture will never form. The development of a leadership culture is done as one step in adapting to a changing world.

A Circle of Impact Leadership culture fosters a vision for impact that can reveal not just a person's or a company's but an entire community's potential for impact. The following story is of one man who created a transformational environment for the people of his company and his city by creating a Circle of Impact Leadership culture.

Creating a Culture of Impact: Craig's Story

Craig owns a local chain of family diners. He competes with the national chains that range from all-day egg and pancake breakfast spots to those specializing in burgers and steaks. He decides early on that anyone can prepare and serve a good meal. He also knows that he can't compete with the marketing dollars that the national chains have to use. So he moves in a different direction. He wants people to come to his restaurant feeling like they are family. He does things to attract families and groups. He has large booths that can seat six to eight people. He has a meeting room in each restaurant that is free for public groups to use. He has recruited and trained his wait staff to personally connect with the public. He wants people to walk into his diners, even for the first time, and feel at home.

Why does he do this? Because he has a vision for impact. After his tenth store reached an expected level of profitability, Craig, along with a few partners, purchased the local minor league baseball team. He negotiated a long-term lease from the city for the ballpark located downtown. Part of their agreement was for the city to invest seed money for mixed-use commercial and residential development around the ballpark. He built a diner adjacent to the stadium that would operate twenty-four hours a day, seven days a week. His purpose for impact was not just to grow more stores. He had a larger vision of impact for his city.

Craig's number one core value was energy. To him, personal energy was the positive force in the universe. He hired people with energy. He put his most energetic folks on the front line with customers. He wanted his diners to be full of happy, positive energy. He believed that if they liked the food and it was priced right, they would come back more often.

Craig negotiated a new promotional agreement with the team's major league parent club. Once each month during the season, a retired player would come to town to conduct pregame youth baseball skills training.

Craig's vision was not to be a minor league baseball owner. It was a step towards something more significant for his city. His vision had to do with the future of his city, and especially as it was tied to its young people.

When Craig took over the team, the minor league park was old, rundown, and not well configured for any other sports. However, behind the ballpark was a large vacant field where a factory once stood. His plan was to create a sports complex with an updated, modern baseball park and a soccer complex next to it.

Craig's plan was to take this one corner of his city and revitalize it. He created several program initiatives to do this. There was the baseball team and renovated ballpark. His new diner. The soccer park focused on the health and fitness of kids. As it developed, he planned to bring a minor league soccer team to play in the ballpark that had been reconfigured to allow for new uses. Craig was creating a center of energy in his home city.

This vision came to Craig because he listened to the people who worked for him. At each of his restaurants, Craig had monthly meetings with the staff. He came there to listen, to learn, and to let their energy feed his drive for impacting his community.

The transition point for Craig came when some of the women who worked for him spoke about the difficult time their sons and daughters were having finding good jobs that would keep them in the city. As Craig sat and listened, and asked some questions, his vision of impact began to form. He knew that his first step was to create a center of energy in the middle of the city. It had to be one that would attract people to come into the city. From that, the new diner, the minor league ball team, and the soccer complex all begin to take shape.

Craig then decided that it wasn't enough to create new jobs in the city. He decided to create a business academy to teach young people the basics of operating a business. His vision was to find young people from his city, who had energy and drive but few opportunities, and mentor and train them in the skills of operating a business. He did not do this on his own. He created a nonprofit organization that brought together the local business and education communities to participate in its programs. Craig knew that if he could find people of energy who lacked the skills they needed to succeed, he could train them. He was known to say, *"Business is hard, but it isn't impossible when you have energy."*

Craig is a Circle of Impact Leader. His diners are Circle of Impact restaurants. His ball team is filled with Circle of Impact baseball players. His soccer complex is filled with Circle of Impact youth soccer teams. His business academy is producing Circle of Impact business leaders of the future.

Craig's approach to business leadership was to see how far his reach could go in making a difference in his community. One of the core principles of Circle of Impact Leadership is to start small to grow big. Craig did just this, starting with one diner, and now has a host of enterprises that are impacting the life of his city because he took personal initiative to make a difference. All along, he stayed true to his core values of the importance of people and the creation of a culture of energy. He maintained a simple, practical plan that anyone could understand and he shared that with everyone he met. Craig's vision saw beyond the moment, beyond the structure of his many endeavors, to see people impacted for the better in his home city. His legacy is the creation of a culture within his community where people could learn, grow, participate, and contribute to making their city a better place to live.

This is a picture of the full potential of a Circle of Impact Leadership culture. This is only the first generation, Craig's generation, of what is possible for a person or a group to achieve when they align themselves for impact. This is the promise of Circle of Impact Leadership: that anyone, regardless of who they are, can take personal initiative, one step at a time, and change the world.

Creating a Culture for Leadership

1. Are you a Circle of Impact Leader? What is the impact that you would most like to create if you could right now?

2. What is the main obstacle that keeps you from taking the first step of initiative?

3. Who do you trust that could join you in your efforts to make a difference that matters? Why don't you invite them to join you?

ACTING LOCALLY
ON A GLOBAL SCALE

Every Place Is a Local Place

Two people from opposite ends of the earth, with nothing in common, and yet, in a moment of gratitude, all those differences faded away. The irony of this moment was that I had traveled halfway around the world to make a difference in the lives of refugees, and here I was finding that this man was making a difference in my life. This man pictured on the following page is my constant reminder that personal leadership always takes place in someone's local community.

The story of this experience from long ago grounds me in the importance of the local character of our personal initiatives to create impact. Our encounter lasted maybe two minutes on a hot afternoon in July 1981. It was an encounter that still impacts me to this day. The man, pictured here, was an Afghan refugee who fled with his family from their home in Afghanistan, across the Khyber Pass, onto a desert plain of the North-West Frontier

The Afghan refugee who honored me.

Province of Pakistan. They were innocent victims of a military conflict between his home country and the Soviet Union. On this day, our small team of refugee workers brought food, clothing, and tents to his impoverished settlement of families.

I never learned his name, but he walked up to me with a smile on his face, took both my hands in his and shook them. He then reached up and stroked the beard on my face. I was too young at that time to appreciate what had happened. Later that day over dinner, Gordon, the leader of our group, told me that he had thanked me in a traditional Afghan manner of one man honoring another man.

His expression of gratitude impacted me in two ways. To be honored by his act of gratitude had an indelible impression upon me about how people of differing cultures can find peace and harmony. At the same time, my perception of the world changed. This experience reminded me that every place is someone's local community. When we connect with one another at a local level, the world changes.

Several years ago, the conversation that I had with an online community of leaders about morale in the workplace was about a topic relevant to each of us in the localness of our lives. As a globally dispersed collection of people, we worked together as a decentralized network of relationships. Even years later, our network remains alive. Whatever is the trending social media spectacle of the day is not where our relationships exist. We are connected by relationships that are local in character and global in scope.

We are an example of an emerging global force of people connected together, crossing social, economic, and national boundaries to create impact. This is a Circle of Impact community model.

Changing Structures

A century ago, at the end of the First World War, the League of Nations was formed as the first global institution. It was formed out of a belief that the nations of the world were not individually capable of avoiding another world war and creating global prosperity. The belief that joining together as a world community that we could overcome the problems of development was one of the great ideas of the modern age. Looking back a century later, we can see that the ideal that created these institutions has yet to be fulfilled. While global prosperity has spread, the violence of war and revolution produced one hundred million casualties worldwide. Today, global institutions of governance and finance are under increasing pressure as the complexity of the world grows. The world's nations are more prosperous, more diverse, more divided, and more difficult to govern than in recent history. Technology is an important factor in changing the context of relationships between people, organizations, and nations on a global scale. Old structures were dependent upon people following a select, elite group of capable leaders. Now, ethnic groups, nations, and individuals are seeking their own prominence. The age of simply following those who are leaders is in transition to a more decentralized world.

This transition that our world is in is unique in human history. If we were to go back in time three or four millennia, we would find that the phenomenon of few leaders and many followers has been the same up until our time. Leadership once was the domain of a king or a queen, a tribal chief, a military ruler, a president, or, in the modern world of corporate businesses, the Chief Executive Officer. Throughout the centuries, organizational leaders were the ones who had the best access to the resources needed to lead. Money, military power, intelligence information, administrative structures, and material resources secured the role of leader. Everyone else became followers or subjects of the ruler. Even as aristocratic regimes transitioned to democracies, the ruling structure of nations remained relatively the same.

Then the digital age emerged, and as it has developed, the resources for leadership began to be dispersed as the cost of distribution dropped. It is not an accident that the age of entrepreneurial business development has accompanied the computer revolution. An individual with a computer and an online account can, from almost any locale in the world, create a thriving business. The proliferation of small businesses selling every possible consumer item online is a mark that the decentralization of commerce is rapidly moving forward.

Decentralized networks of relationships are the new context for human engagement. They have a very different structure. They are more agile, can more quickly change their products, develop new services, and shift marketing strategies overnight if needed. This decentralization of power is placing greater stress upon the legacy institutions that depended upon centralized control to maintain their prominence in the marketplace.

In a centralized world, structure is the organization of the basic facets of any business of governance, finance, products/ programs, and operations. If the organization is out of alignment of the kind that is modeled by the Circle of Impact, the company suffers.

A decentralized structure is organized to maximize the interaction that takes place among people. The alignment fostered by the Circle of Impact creates the network effects that come with a leader-rich, impact-centric purpose.

These are not competing structural systems, but complimentary ones. The transition that we are in is not a rejection of centralized structures, but of their modification through the implementation of networks of relationships. This is why the Circle of Impact model of leadership and alignment meets a critical need for organizations of all types. It is making possible the rise of local action on a global scale.

My experience that afternoon in the refugee camp in Pakistan showed me that we all live in local communities. Add that perspective to our always-on connection to the internet, and we can live in meaningful connection every day. All networks of relationships are local networks. When Raj in Mumbai consults with Kenji in Tokyo on his presentation to a French electronics company, their conversation is about a specific need that Kenji has. Their relationship has become a local one, operating in a virtual space rather than a physical one.

The future is both personal and social. In the social, we find Circle of Impact Leaders bridging the organizational divide between hierarchy and networks, between centralized structures and decentralized ones. When the network of relationships becomes the culture of leadership in a company, the local impact of these relationships can the reach a global scale. The future in this regard is a relational one.

Why Local Matters

Former Speaker of the U.S. House of Representatives Tip O'Neill was famous for saying that *"all politics is local."* When he said this nearly a half century ago, it was before our internet-connected world had developed. During my summer of refugee work in Pakistan, I'd write a letter home, posting it from our base in the hill town of Murree, and, a week later it would arrive home. Today, I can have a face-to-face conversation with my daughter, who lives in China. We no longer talk about making long-distance calls. All calls are local.

Our perception of the world and our place in it is changing. Three decades ago, I sat with my father's father, whom we called Pappy, as we celebrated the birth of my first son. We are all named after him. Pappy was born in the late 19th century in a small Piedmont North Carolina, county-seat town. He lived into his mid-90s. He saw the dramatic changes of the 20th century up close. As we sat with his namesake on his lap, I asked him, *"What was the most significant change that you've seen during your life?"* Without hesitating, he answered, *"The radio!"* I asked him why. *"Because we found out that people lived elsewhere."* From the wireless transmissions of my grandfather's childhood radio that connected the stories of people in one place with listeners in another, we have not really traveled that far to the instantaneous communication on our smartphones today. The impact of this change is that we have the power to connect globally in a personal, one-to-one, more mutually beneficial way than ever.

Today, we are not bound by the geography of what is local. Instead, we are free to choose to have global relationships that impact us on a local level. Our lives are no longer just about our town, the street we live on, or the people we meet on the bus or at the market. Local is relational. When it becomes more personal and relational for us, we can then take personal initiative to have an impact on the other side of the world because it makes a difference to someone who now matters to us. This is why the most significant change we go through is in our self-perception. Can you see yourself as a local leader of impact whose story inspires others around the world to follow your example? This is the future that is opening to you and me.

The possibilities that come when we decide to be engaged locally far from home is the next step after we become locally impactful. Here's a story of two of my closest friends who have inspired me.

Impacting Locally Far from Home:
David and Donna's Story

The inspiration for this chapter comes from two of my friends who live this idea of having a global impact at a local level. David and Donna Pu'u live in a California coastal town where they can surf every day. David is an artist with a fascinatingly varied career. Donna owns Betty Belts, an "ocean-inspired" jewelry and apparel brand. She has a passion for surfing that is second to none. Years ago, Donna went to Bali, Indonesia, to find artisans for her designs. She connected with Balinese locals. One couple she met had a jewelry business. They introduced her to the silver artisans with whom she now works to create her jewelry.

This is the way things can happen. Connections are made. Relationships form. Mutual benefit is discovered. Businesses grow. Communities develop, become stronger, healthier, more resilient, and successful. Children grow up prepared to live in a globally connected world of relationships. This is what is taking place in Bali with David and Donna, because a faraway, dream place to surf became a local place to do business and invest in the people who lived there.

The vision that I want you to see is that the world doesn't have to be a far distant place, detached from us, just a collection of images in a book or on a computer screen. Feeling empathy and compassion, but doing nothing in response, is not just unsatisfying, it produces a sense of regret. Even writing may not be sufficient to fulfill in us a desire to make a difference. Acting locally is not about making us feel good and noble. It is instead about having an impact in the local community of our choice. The personal cannot find true fulfillment until it becomes the social, which is always a product of the quality of our relationships.

Today, we are no longer limited by geography. We no longer have to live a life as an observer of other people's lives. We can step out and choose to move toward a life of meaningful connection with people and places who can benefit from what we have to offer. In return our lives are transformed by honor and gratitude, with a vision of impact that we see being lived out right in front of us.

Many times I've sat in David and Donna's home, watching her take beautiful pieces of sea glass and design a jewelry setting, which then goes to the silver artisans in Bali. Her Balinese artisans are not faraway nameless/faceless people working in a sweat shop. They are people with families that she knows, and her California business provides them jobs which support their families. But that is not the extent of their connection.

When a human being has a name, they become a person, with a story to tell that connects us with them in their local setting. When we decide that these relationships matter, we begin to think about what our responsibility to them may be. When we discover that they have something to offer us in return that is meaningful, like the Afghan refugee father who honored me with gratitude, the connection that we have globally at a local level changes the world.

Over the years, Donna and David's relationships with the people of Bali has grown beyond the particulars of a business relationship and a love for surfing. An introduction to a British ex-patriot named David Booth brought them into a relationship with the people who live in the mountain villages at the eastern end of the island. Booth, nearly two decades ago, became concerned about these village people. He formed the East Bali Poverty Project to address the challenges and opportunities that he sees there. Their mission statement reads: *To eliminate poverty and promote culturally sensitive, sustainable social and economic development in the impoverished rural communities of East Bali, Indonesia, prioritizing the health, nutrition, and education of children.*

Donna, moved by Booth's vision and the impact that he is having, has designated his organization as her business's recipient of the *"1% for the Planet"* contribution. When they can, they visit with Booth and the people in the mountain villages they are now supporting. For Donna and David, Bali is a part of their local community. They spend part of each year there working with the silver artisans, surfing with local kids, and investing in development projects with the people in the mountain villages. For them, Bali is not a tourist destination. It is part of their local community, and the people are part of their family.

The Local Is Now

When we hear stories like that of David and Donna's connection to Bali, it warms our hearts and we feel deep appreciation for what they are doing. But, too often, we don't take the next step to ask, *"Why not me?"*

You may ask, where do I start? You don't have to travel to Bali to find a local community worth caring for. Within a few miles of your home or business are people who would benefit from a relationship with you. Don't start with a project. Start just with getting to know one another. Because what may happen is that they are not the object of a local community relationship, but you are.

A long time ago I heard a Scottish professor speak about going to his first American football game. He said the stadium was full, the crowd energetic, and the game exciting. He said that they went to the game to cheer and elevate their team to a win. To his surprise, he found that he was elevated. I think this often happens when we place ourselves in a position of developing a relationship with someone who is not from our neighborhood, town, or nation. My experience with the Afghan refugee taught me that.

Whenever we take personal initiative to create impact, we are leading the way for others to join us. When we do, we find that leadership is not just personal, but social. When the social works, the impact can be magical. Just ask David and Donna.

Leading as a Local Organization

Many of the stories of people that I have met, who are taking personal initiative for leadership impact on a local level, are doing so as individuals. It is also true that every healthy local community is so because there are local businesses and organizations that are also taking initiative to strengthen their local community.

A weak, poorly functioning business is not just weak for itself, but for the community as a whole. A business is not just a collection of purposeful activities. It is also a social context that strengthens the community. This is what Craig, the owner of local diners, a minor league baseball team, and the creator of the soccer complex, understood. His local impact touched the lives of people who live in his town, as well as those who came as tourists and business travelers.

From a local base, global impact can be achieved. However, it must begin at home, so that what we have to offer the world is strong and sustainable. This is how the Circle of Impact moves from being a model illustrated on a screen to being a guide for us to take personal initiative to make a difference one global locality at a time.

This is the future of leadership. And the future of our lives, where we discover that we have yet to truly tap into the potential for goodness that remains hidden until we act.

START SMALL, GROW BIG

It is my aim to live past a hundred years old. Both my grand-fathers lived to ninety-four years old, so I think I have a chance.

I was talking about personal leadership and living to a hundred with a group of high school students in Vienna, Austria.

"How many of you are bored?"

Several raised their hands.

"You know that with the advances in modern medicine and healthy living most of you could easily live past a hundred years old."

I then asked, how many were born in the year 2000? Probably a third of the hundred students in the room raised their hands.

"I want you to think about waking up on January 1, 2100, and reflecting back on your life. If you are bored now, will you be bored then? I hope not."

Most of us don't think in these terms. We are increasingly told to live in the present. The future is just too big for us to grasp. Enjoy the day.

Except I think we end up never really seeing the potential that we had as young people. I have several men and women in mind who were mentors to me when they were past retirement age, and I was still young and clueless. None of those people made it to a hundred. But if I make it there, their legacy of influence will.

I said to the students that one of the reasons we find life boring is that we measure it by our activities. I did this and that today. And tomorrow I'll go there. After a few weeks or years, all we have to show for our lives are a full calendar and some interesting stories to tell.

I suggested to the students that they should order their lives around the impact they could have. I asked, *"How many of you are making a difference in some one's life right now?"*

A young man sitting in the front row raised his hand. I had him stand up and tell us what he is doing. He told us that he is mentoring a middle-school student. He said it with such joy and energy, you could tell he would live a long life of making a difference in people's lives.

I then turned the discussion back to the length of their lives.

"Did you know that if you are seventeen right now, you would live another eighty-three years if you make it to 100? Do you know how many days are in eighty-three years? Over 30,000 days.

"Now, I want you to consider making a decision today, that you will try every day for the rest of your life to do something that makes a difference that matters. As you reach 100 in 2100, you can look back on your life and all those 30,000 moments of impact will come flying back through your mind.

"If you do this, how many of you think your life will be boring?"

Being a person of impact doesn't take a massively big change in your life. It just starts with something small. Maybe you take someone to lunch, and you talk about their challenges in life. Or maybe you stay after work and help someone finish putting the conference packets together. All you do is start. Start small and do something every day.

As I stood there in the high school library, looking at the bright future of the world, I wondered if I had made a difference to them. I decided to push my idea about living a life of impact to a ridiculous level.

"I am assuming that since all of you are business students, that you understand how to organize things. I want you to think about organizing your life around the impact that you can create.

"Now if you have 30,000 days ahead of you, and the potential for 30,000 moments of impact, why don't you organize your life and work so that you can create a moment of impact every hour of every day for the rest of your life? After all, you will be doing something every hour for the rest of your life. Why not make each hour an hour for impact? We are now talking about you having 720,000 moments of impact in your life. Imagine the difference your life will have made by simply deciding today that you will live a life of impact."

To live this way begins with a change in our self-perception. Most of us have not been raised to think this way. Rather, we have been taught the opposite. Don't extend yourself. Be conservative. Don't risk. Avoid disappointment. Play by the rules. Don't stand out. Just fit in.

This well-meaning advice comes from our elders who don't want us to experience the hardship and disappointment that many of them faced.

I've learned to do the opposite. To constantly try new things. Failing is not trying. Even when I decided to start my life over, I never thought about failing. I just thought about getting up every day and trying.

This is why I believe that we should start small and work our way up to *big*.

I knew that I had the attention of the students and the faculty that were in the room. So, I took it up a notch.

"Since this is a business high school, I am assuming that you are learning about how to scale a business. Correct?"

No response.

I looked over at one of the professors and smiled.

"Okay. Let me suggest that you learn how to scale a business. I want you to learn this so you can learn how to scale your impact.

"What I mean is that I want you intentionally to organize every facet of your life so that you create a moment of impact... every minute of every hour of every day, for the rest of your life.

"Someone do the math. How many moments of impact are we talking about?"

Silence.

"We're talking about forty-five million moments of impact."

Now I know this is a ridiculous proposition to place before these students. But it is only ridiculous because we have been told that it is.

"How many students are here at your school?"

Several students speak up. *"One thousand."*

"Okay. Now I want you to imagine that each of you during your lifetime in some way touch the lives of forty-five million people. What if all one thousand of you had this kind of life? It would mean this one school in Vienna, Austria, would have changed course of human history."

In the absurdity of these large numbers is a truth that I want you to reflect upon. No one knows what is possible in the future. No one. You don't. I don't. All we have is the opportunity today to make a difference that matters. Then we'll have the same opportunity tomorrow. And the day after.

Leading a life of impact doesn't start big, but small.

When I started my life over, my only goal was to write a book. I started one. Not this one. My editor told me that it wasn't very good. She said, *"Do something with your leadership model, the Circle of Impact."* So, I began. Day one. Day two. Until today.

At some point in this process, I began to think big. I started small, but then I went big.

My aim was to inspire and equip people to take personal initiative to create impact that makes a difference that matters in their local communities.

My first *big* thought was to move one percent of the population of the United States to take leadership initiative. I had that vision three years ago. One percent was about three million people. Then a friend said, *"Why do you limit yourself?"* That's funny. Three million people, a limited number.

She challenged me to look at the whole world. Everyone everywhere needs to be encouraged to become a Circle of Impact Leader. Okay. One percent of the world's population.

That is around seventy-three million people. Wow! Now we are talking about some *big* numbers.

Then I heard another friend speak about how he had 10Xed his company. He spoke about growing our business by ten times. As he spoke, I thought, *"Okay. What's ten percent of the world's population...? Wow! 730 million people."*

Now that is a truly ridiculous number. Until it is not.

My challenge to you is to do something today that you did not plan to do that makes a difference in somebody's life. Start to become a Circle of Impact Leader today. Start small. Act locally. Be patient. Find the joy in doing things that create impact. Keep a record of what you are doing. Create a story. Your story. It is the story that you tell yourself about why the personal initiative you take matters. Once you start, and you begin to pick up momentum, then begin to dream big about what is possible if you organize and scale your impact.

One last thing to remember: Circle of Impact Leadership is both personal and social. You take initiative, and if you need help, you can find me at my website, edbrenegar.com.